The DNA *of* SUCCESS

Incredible stories
from the worlds of
business, politics,
the military,
sport & the arts

CHRIS NORTON

The DNA of Success
© Chris Norton

ISBN: 978-1-906316-66-2

Published in 2011 by HotHive Books, Evesham, UK.
www.thehothive.com

The right of Chris Norton to be identified as the author of this work has
been asserted by him in accordance with the Copyright, Designs and
Patents Act 1988.

A CIP record of this book is available from the British Library.

Printed in the UK by TJ International, Padstow.

The DNA *of* SUCCESS

Incredible stories from the worlds
of business, politics, the military, sport &
the arts

Contents

Acknowledgements

At this stage I would like to thank our contributors, who have given so freely of their time, experience and expertise to help make *The DNA of Success* happen: Lord (Ian) MacLaurin, Vince Cable, Baroness (Brenda) Dean, Greg Dyke, Frederick Forsyth CBE, Penny Hughes CBE, Sir Peter Squire and Graham Taylor OBE. My thanks also go to Mahan Khalsa, a world-renowned expert in business development and business-to-business sales, who has worked with me and allowed me to use the 'intelligence tools' to graphically bring to life practical applications.

It is very rare in life that you can say that something would not have happened without the work of one person, but I can definitely say that in this case – and that person is Sally Hennessy. Sally is a remarkable individual who has worked with many of the best business leaders and spent ten years in business as executive assistant to Lord MacLaurin. Sally has been instrumental in helping me organise and make *The DNA of Success* happen, and while it's not explicitly called out in the book you will see many instances of where powerful, productive women have made a massive difference to the success of the people and the companies they work with. Sally is among those individuals, and I thank her very much for her help and friendship.

In terms of the production of the book … thanks to my publishers, the HotHive, who have been fantastic in terms of real value-added help and advice, in particular Sara and Karen – both superstars in the world of publishing, in my view! Within the HotHive team was Mark Hobin, who designed the cover that has consistently received great feedback and Lorna Coombs, the copy editor who definitely earned her money! Also thanks to Carina Newton, from my company Mentor Group, who helped decipher my notes and writing.

Also, my thanks and love go to my wife, Ines, and my eight-year-old daughter, Lara, for being fantastically supportive of me in the writing of this book. They have been sufficiently inspired to have both started writing books of their own. In terms of my success, they are absolutely a key part of my motivation and I consider myself blessed to have them in my life.

About the author

Chris Norton is a director of Mentor Group and Chairman of Watford FC Community Sports and Education Trust.

Chris lives in Twickenham with his wife, Ines, and eight-year-old daughter, Lara – a keen gymnast who is already training for the 2016 Olympics! He combines his busy business life with outside interests, including football, sport in general, and his family both in the UK and Brazil – his wife's former home.

Chris is a lifelong fan of Watford Football Club, having been born and educated in Watford and later at Hatfield Polytechnic, now the University of Hertfordshire. He is currently a director of Mentor Group, a global training and coaching consultancy, having previously held senior positions at Dell Computer Corporation and Honeywell. His first book, *Bare Knuckle Customer Service,* was published in 2008 and *The DNA of Success* is his second book.

The ethos behind this book is to find the real person behind the success story. By linking personalities from business, politics, the military, sport and the arts, Chris gives his readers an insight into what makes these people different. The book focuses on key themes around leadership, achievement, success and, probably just as importantly, setbacks and difficulties and how success has emerged in different ways for each individual. To link his work as an author with his passion for Watford FC Community Sports and Education Trust, Chris will be donating a percentage of the profits from the sales of the book to this charity.

As part of his role as a director of Mentor Group, Chris has worked with and coached leaders in major global corporations, and one of the main strengths of this book is the combination of Chris's business knowledge and experience with his life experience and associations with sport, politics and the arts.

In terms of his role with the Trust at Watford FC, Chris is passionate about using his experience in sales, customer service, training and coaching to make a difference to how the Trust operates and delivers on its promises to the community. The aims of the Trust are to make a difference in young people's lives through sport and learning. In 2009 the Trust helped no fewer than 120,000 young people and adults – an amazing achievement. In 2010 this was exceeded, with 149,000 people passing through the Trust's activities. It was also a landmark year for the Trust, with the first brick being laid for a new £5m facility in Harrow, Middlesex: the site for a community hub offering a full range of sporting and leisure facilities run through Watford FC's Trust as a major social inclusion initiative.

Contributor biographies

Ian Charter MacLaurin

Ian Charter MacLaurin, Baron MacLaurin of Knebworth, DL (born 30 March 1937) is a British businessman who has been chairman of two highly successful organisations – namely, Vodafone and Tesco. He is a former chairman of the England and Wales Cricket Board, a former chancellor of the University of Hertfordshire and a supporter/patron of several charities, including the cricket charity 'A Chance to Shine' and the cancer charity 'Hope for Tomorrow'.

Lord MacLaurin joined Tesco in 1959 as a management trainee, and then held a number of more senior appointments in its retail operations before being appointed to its board in 1970. He became managing director in the 1970s and chairman in 1985.

By the time of his retirement in 1997, Tesco had overtaken Sainsbury's to become the largest UK retailer. Lord MacLaurin led Tesco away from the 'pile it high, sell it cheap' business philosophy of founder Jack Cohen. He has claimed that one of his most important acts was appointing the right successor, Sir Terry Leahy, and subsequently another of his management trainees, Phil Clarke, who took over from Sir Terry this year.

Lord MacLaurin joined Vodafone as a non-executive director in 1997, becoming chairman in July 1998. He briefly stepped down on the merger with AirTouch Communications Inc. in 1999, and resumed his role a year later. When he stepped down from the main Vodafone board in July 2006, he became an adviser to the company. He was succeeded as chairman by Sir John Bond. He then became chairman of the Vodafone Group Foundation, an independent charitable trust set up to administer charitable and other donations on behalf of the company throughout the world.

Among other commitments, Lord MacLaurin was chairman of the Sport Honours Committee and the board of Heineken until earlier this year. He has served on the board of the bank Evolution Securities plc for nine years and also served as a non-executive director of Whitbread and NatWest.

He is still chairman of the council of his old school, Malvern College. He is married to Paula and they live near Bath. He has kindly agreed to write the foreword to this book.

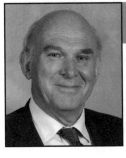

John Vincent 'Vince' Cable

John Vincent 'Vince' Cable (born 9 May 1943) is a British Liberal Democrat politician who is currently the Secretary of State for Business, Innovation and skills in the coalition cabinet of David Cameron. He has been Member of Parliament for Twickenham since 1997.

Cable studied Economics at university and became an economic adviser to the Kenyan government in 1966. He was an adviser to the British government and to the Commonwealth Secretary-General in the 1970s and 1980s.

Later, he served as chief economist for the oil company Shell from 1995 to 1997. In the 1970s, Cable was active in the Labour Party and became a Glasgow councillor. However, in 1982 he joined the Social Democratic Party, which would go on to form the Liberal Democrats, and he unsuccessfully contested seats in the elections of 1983, 1987 and 1992 until eventually being elected as the MP for the London constituency of Twickenham in the 1997 general election.

He was the Liberal Democrats' main economic spokesperson from 2003 to May 2010 and he was elected deputy leader in March 2006, and following Sir Menzies Campbell's resignation, he was acting leader for two months – from October 2007 until the election of Nick Clegg. He resigned from his position as deputy leader in May 2010. He has had a high profile since the global financial crisis of 2007–10 and has written several books on economics and trade.

Cable is one of the Liberal Democrats' best minds and most capable parliamentary practitioners. Yet he was little known outside the party until relatively recently, partly because, during his first term as an MP, he divided his time between Westminster and nursing his late beloved wife, Olympia, an erudite woman of Indian descent, until she died of cancer. "It left me with a lifelong admiration for carers," he says.

For many years, he has been going twice a week to a dancing school in Hampton Wick for lessons in ballroom and Latin dancing. On YouTube, there's a clip of him twirling around the dance floor with *Strictly Come Dancing* winner, Alesha Dixon. "He clearly knows his steps. He enjoys what he does. He looks like he's not afraid of a bit of hard work," says Dixon. In 2008 Vince married again, having proposed to a lady farmer named Rachel from near Brockenhurst in the New Forest. Fortunately Rachel is also a keen dancer.

Brenda Dean

Brenda Dean, Baroness Dean of Thornton-le-Fylde (born 29 April 1943) began her career as a trade unionist as a teenager and was elected as general president of the print union SOGAT in 1983 and general secretary in 1985. She was the first British woman to lead a major craft or industrial trade union.

She became a life peer in October 1993 as Baroness Dean of Thornton-le-Fylde, of Eccles in the County of Greater Manchester, and a Privy Councillor in 1998.

Baroness Dean has been a member of numerous public bodies and committees, and served as vice-chair of the University College London Hospitals NHS Trust from 1994 until 1998, when she was appointed to chair the Housing Corporation. She is currently serving her second three-year term as chair of Covent Garden Market Authority, a post she has held since 1 April 2005.

She is the author of *Hot Mettle*, an autobiography dealing largely with the period when she was general secretary of SOGAT at the time of Rupert Murdoch's battles with that and other trade unions. She is a Fellow of the Royal Society of Arts and has chaired several committees in the House of Lords.

Baroness Dean is married to Keith McDowell CBE, ex-deputy director-general of the CBI and ex-industrial editor of the *Daily Mail*, and they live in London and Cornwall.

Greg Dyke

Greg Dyke (born May 1947) was educated at Hayes Grammar School, after which he worked briefly for Marks & Spencer and as a reporter for the *Hillingdon Mirror* before gaining admission to the University of York as a mature student, with one grade E at A level, and graduating with a BA in Politics – ironically, he is now the university's chancellor. After university, Dyke moved into journalism and was also public relations spokesperson for the Wandsworth Council for Community Relations.

He then worked for London Weekend Television (LWT) before taking a job at TV-am in 1993, where he was instrumental in reviving the breakfast show's fortunes by introducing Roland Rat, a hand puppet, to liven up the show. Following TV-am, he became director of programmes for Television South (TVS), and later returned to LWT, making a fortune when Granada bought out the firm. Stints at Pearson Television and Channel 5 followed.

In 2000 he took over the helm of the BBC from John Birt. At the beginning of his tenure he famously promised to "cut the crap" at the corporation. The "crap" he referred to was the complex internal market Birt had introduced at the BBC which, it is claimed, turned employees away from making programmes and into managers. He reversed this trend by reducing administration costs from 24% of total income to 15%. Unusually for a recent Director General, he had a good rapport with his employees and was well liked by the majority of BBC staff.

Apart from restoring staff morale, Dyke laid claim to two major achievements during his term of office. In 2002 he introduced the Freeview terrestrial digital transmission platform with six additional BBC channels, and persuaded Sky TV to join the consortium. After leaving the BBC, he said that he always realised that the introduction of Freeview helped to prevent a subscription funding model for the BBC to gain traction, because it is impossible for broadcasters to switch off the signal to individual Freeview boxes. He resigned from the BBC on 29 January 2004, after the publication of the Hutton Report in which Hutton described Dyke's approach to checking news stories as "defective".

In November 2003, Dyke was formally appointed by the University of York as its new chancellor. There was some controversy regarding his appointment in the midst of the Iraq Dossier scandal. He officially took up the post in August 2004. In this role, he is the honorific and ceremonial head of the university, as well as heading the University Development Board. He has also made a personal grant to the new Department of Theatre, Film and Television, to fund the Greg Dyke Chair in Film and Television.

In 2004 Dyke announced that he had signed a six-figure book contract with HarperCollins. The book, *Inside Story*, subsequently published in September 2004, goes into detail about his opinion on the relationship between the BBC and the British government, and of the Dr David Kelly affair and the Hutton Inquiry. He was appointed chair of the British Film Institute in February 2008.

Dyke is a serious fan of Brentford FC and was appointed as non-executive chairman of the club on 20 January 2006, following the takeover by the Brentford Supporters' Trust, Bees United. He had previously served on the board at Manchester United as a non-executive director from 1997 to 1999. He is married to Sue Howes and they have four children.

Frederick Forsyth
[Photo: Gill Shaw]

Frederick Forsyth CBE

Frederick Forsyth CBE (born 25 August 1938) is a leading English author best known for thrillers such as *The Day of the Jackal, The Odessa File, The Fourth Protocol, The Dogs of War, The Devil's Alternative, The Fist of God, Icon, The Veteran, Avenger, The Afghan* and *The Cobra*.

The son of a furrier, Forsyth was born in Ashford, Kent. He was educated at Tonbridge School and later attended the University of Granada in Spain. At the age of 19, he became one of the youngest pilots in the Royal Air Force, where he did national service from 1956 to 1958. He joined Reuters in 1961 and later the

BBC in 1965, where he was made an assistant diplomatic correspondent. From July to September 1967, he was sent as a correspondent to cover the Nigerian Civil War between the region of Biafra and the Nigerian government. He left the BBC in 1968 after controversy arose over his alleged bias towards the Biafran cause. Returning to Biafra as a freelance reporter, Forsyth wrote his first book, *The Biafra Story*, in 1969. He speaks fluent French, German and Spanish, and has travelled widely throughout Europe, the Middle East, Africa, North America, Asia, Australia and New Zealand and these experiences can be seen in the authenticity of his books.

Forsyth is a Eurosceptic Conservative and is patron of Better Off Out, an organisation calling for Britain's withdrawal from the European Union. He is a strong supporter of the British monarchy, and in his book *Icon* he recommends a constitutional monarchy as a solution to Russia's political problems following the collapse of the Soviet Union. In October 2010, Forsyth was shortlisted for the Bigot of the Year award in the 2010 Stonewall Awards.

He lives in Hertfordshire with his wife, Sandy.

Penny Hughes CBE

Penny Hughes CBE (born 1959) is a British businesswoman.

Hughes was educated at Birkenhead High School, where she represented the county at tennis and lacrosse and developed a lifelong love of sport. She was awarded a first-class degree in Chemistry from Sheffield University and soon after graduating she joined Procter & Gamble as a technologist, then moved to the sales and marketing department.

She was then recruited by the Milk Marketing Board, and later joined Coca-Cola as a brand manager. By 1989, having successfully overseen the merger of the marketing interests of Coca-Cola UK and Schweppes, she was appointed commercial director and in 1993, at the age of 33, she became the youngest and only woman to become president of the UK and Ireland businesses of Coca-Cola. She left Coca-Cola in 1995.

Hughes has been a director of the Bodyshop, Gap, Trinity Mirror, Next, Skandinaviska Enskilda Banken, Vodafone and Reuters and on 1 January 2010 she took up a non-executive directorship with Royal Bank of Scotland Group, where she chairs the board's remuneration committee. She is currently a non-executive director of Morrisons, Cable & Wireless and Home Retail Group. She is also a trustee of the British Museum and president of the Advertising Association.

Hughes has two teenage sons and is married to David. They live in Teddington, where she skilfully balances her busy family life with her extensive and demanding business interests. Apparently, she is also a real ale fan and a loyal supporter of Liverpool FC.

In June 2011 Penny was awarded a CBE for services to media for work as President of the Advertising Association over a period of six years.

Sir Peter Squire

Air Chief Marshal **Sir Peter Squire** GCB, DFC, AFC, DL, DSc, FRAeS (born 7 October 1945) is a retired senior Royal Air Force commander. He was a fast-jet pilot in the 1970s and a senior officer in the 1980s. He was a squadron commander during the Falklands War and a senior commander in the 1990s. He was Chief of the Air Staff from 2000 to 2003 and aide-de-camp to HM the Queen from 1999 to 2003.

Sir Peter was appointed commanding officer of No. 1 (F) Squadron based at RAF Wittering in 1981, flying Harriers. In 1982 he led members of his squadron in action in the Falklands campaign, for which he was awarded the DFC. He flew with his squadron to CFB Goose Bay in Canada on 13 April 1982, where they embarked with their aircraft aboard the *Atlantic Conveyor*. On 13 June, he was the first member of the RAF to launch a laser-guided bomb in combat. Four Harriers from his squadron of ten were lost, three to ground fire and one after an engine failure led to a heavy landing. His squadron was also the first to operate in a combat role from a British aircraft carrier since the Second World War. Later in the year, on 6 November, he was forced to eject near Cape Pembroke in the Falklands due to a Harrier's engine failure.

He became leader of the Command Briefing and Presentation Team in 1984 and then went on to be Personal Staff Officer to the Air Officer Commanding RAF Strike Command. Promoted to Group Captain in 1985, he took up the appointment of Station Commander of RAF Cottesmore in 1986.

Promoted to Air Commodore in 1989, he became Director Air Offensive at the Ministry of Defence in 1989, and following his promotion to Air Vice-Marshal, he became Senior Air Staff Officer at HQ Strike Command and Deputy Chief of Staff Operations UK Air Forces in 1991. He then became Air Officer Commanding No. 38 Group.

He was appointed Air Officer Commanding No. 1 Group in February 1993. He served as Assistant Chief of the Air Staff from 1994, as Deputy Chief of Defence Staff (Programmes and Personnel) from 1996 and as Commander-in-Chief RAF Strike Command from 1999. He served as Chief of the Air Staff from 2000 to 2003.

Sir Peter is currently chairman of the board of trustees of the Imperial War Museum and held the position vice-chairman of the board of the Commonwealth War Graves Commission until July 2008. He is also a Deputy Lieutenant of Devon. He is married to Carolyn and they have three sons.

Graham Taylor OBE

Graham Taylor
[Photo: Alan Cozzi]

Graham Taylor OBE (born 15 September 1944 in Worksop, Nottinghamshire) is a football manager and a former player. He is best known as the manager of the England national football team, as well as being manager of Watford, a club he took from the Fourth Division to the First in the space of five years, then from bottom of the Second Division to the Premier League in two seasons two decades later.

Taylor grew up in the industrial steel town of Scunthorpe, where he still has many connections and which he still regards as his hometown. The son of a sports journalist with the *Scunthorpe Evening Telegraph*, Taylor discovered his love of football in the stands of the 'Old Show Ground' watching Scunthorpe United, a team he still supports, and he is often seen at home matches. When growing up, however, Taylor supported Wolves, the team he was later to manage.

The football style played by his teams was often criticised by purists as being focused on the 'long ball' style of getting the ball quickly to physically powerful forwards although, unlike many long ball advocates, Taylor also liked to play with skilful wingers, who could beat defenders, hit the byline and produce dangerous crosses into the opposition's penalty area. In this respect, John Barnes was perhaps the archetypal Taylor player. Although viewed as being aesthetically unattractive by the often-losing opposition, Taylor's style proved incredibly successful in terms of club football, although less so when applied to the more composed pace of the international game. His most recent managerial role was as manager of Aston Villa, whom he left at the end of the 2002–03 season. He now works as a pundit for BBC Radio 5 live and for several years he served as a member of the Sport Honours Committee. Taylor is a supporter of Sense – National Deafblind and Rubella Association and is a patron of DebRA. He is a celebrity ambassador for the Sense Enterprise Board in Birmingham, and has worked to raise both funds and awareness, including by running the London Marathon in 2004. He is currently chairman of Watford FC and is married to Rita – they have two daughters, Joanne and Karen.

Foreword

Ian Charter MacLaurin, Baron MacLaurin of Knebworth, DL

Chris Norton told me that every week three or four books are published on how to be successful in business – so he has been very brave to add this book to that huge list. He knew when he embarked upon this project that it had to be different and it had to approach the subject in an unusual and really interesting way. He had to produce something that had not been done before and, by combining real-life experiences from real people and then backing his theories with solid research, he has managed exactly that.

I have been lucky enough to have enjoyed a long and varied career in retail and sport and I believe that there are many great teachers waiting to tell their stories. Chris has gathered some of the best in the UK in what his readers will, I hope, find a fascinating and unique approach to the DNA of Success.

Chris interviewed this group, all of whom have spoken to him with great honesty and openness about their lives, and he has captured their experiences and stories to accurately illustrate the various themes he covers.

The common denominator in all the interviews – and remember these men and women come from a wide variety of backgrounds including business, sport, literature, the military and politics – is that each individual has a vision, and he or she follows that vision to ultimate achievement.

For me, one of the most fascinating chapters covers transformational setbacks – the inevitable ups and downs of life and work – but these people are not put off by problems, they continue to seek their goals and they learn from their mistakes and move on. Another chapter that will resonate for many readers is that on 'synchronicity' – being in the right place at the right time – and being able to recognise an opportunity when it presents itself and then run with it.

Chris has combined the in-depth interviews with solid research and he gives the reader a full insight into what it has taken for these people to achieve success in their chosen careers. There is much to learn and I believe that Chris has achieved something unique in a 'how to do' book. He has managed to combine a serious learning tool with a thoroughly good read and I am sure that readers will learn a great deal from this very special book – I certainly did!

Over the last 30 years, I have been lucky enough to mix with some remarkable and successful people in the worlds of politics, sport, charity and business. In this time I have met and worked with many outstanding, inspirational and engaging people. These include Michael Dell, who pioneered the direct business model; Graham Taylor, who I believe is one of the few football managers to successfully make the transition between running a football team and running a business; and a whole host of other notable, successful people – some of whom have agreed to be part of this story.

My business interest and personal passion is in people development and I have always been curious about success: the achievement of success, and how we can learn from the best to create the best opportunities for our own success.

In recent years I have coached and carried out extensive studies and research around leadership and management in organisations and successful sales teams. However, it has been the success of individual people within all those environments that has always fascinated me the most. This has prompted me to ask three questions:

- What makes that person successful?
- How do they do it so easily?
- How can we model and replicate this form of success intelligence and share it?

There seems to be a consistent commonality among truly successful people in terms of their way of being, and I have continued to search for a breakthrough and inspiration.

Over time these questions, around success in teams and enabling solutions with clients in the area of sales and leadership, have enabled me to build a very successful business in Mentor Group, providing sales and leadership development for some of the leading global companies. However, this has only added to my curiosity about success and the true secret of success at an individual level.

As always in life, when the timing is right you then meet a particular person, the penny drops, the answer comes and the breakthrough happens. The timing for me was September 2009 and that person was Lord MacLaurin. It was a brief meeting, but at that point my resolve to write this book was born and I am lucky enough to have Lord MacLaurin as a key contributor and writer of the foreword to this book.

From that point onwards I rapidly gathered information and I'm still amazed at the truly wonderful, diverse array of talent that I have been able to include within this book. This has continued to build right up to the last piece of the jigsaw when I secured the services of Mahan Khalsa, founder of Franklin Covey's Sales Performance Division, who truly is a genius in the 'how' and 'how to do' of success.

My end in mind for this book has always been to help people, as at heart I now realise that I have a real drive, determination and passion for making a difference for people through personal development, which is not a statement I would have made in my formative years.

Making a difference in the lives of others is something I love doing, and I hope and trust that my book will be another part of your journey and the progressive realisation of your business and life goals.

In terms of how the book is written, I want to make this different from the tens of thousands of other publications that have been written on success (no fewer than three are published each week!) and I have applied three underlying principles and aims to achieve this difference.

Firstly, I conducted my interviews without carrying out endless research first, so that what I really learnt, understood and translated from the real-life stories of our contributors were the key commonalities and consistencies that helped them to be successful in whatever their walk of life. My role was to question, listen, explore and discover through their great stories, both of success and of setbacks. I did this without tailoring or filtering my approach with research or my own bias, experience and views. This was remarkably successful in hindsight, as those life stories and experiences have built a rich stream of insightful, powerful and consistent streams of knowledge, know-how and insight that I can use in the building of the DNA of Success.

Secondly, I then carried out research to seek confirmation that the criteria for the DNA of Success that I had elicited from my interviews could be supported. I had empirical evidence from my interviews with great people and around great success; now I wanted to match that to research in a wide variety of areas. So the research I carried out was not only within the business community and existing literature, but I also widened it to cover charity and sport and to include key people from among my global clients and their personal insights. Overall, this has given me a wealth of research and background information to share through the book.

Thirdly, and critically important for me, I wanted to include throughout practical tools and applications so that I could give a 'how to do' as well as the 'what to do' in terms of helping people to achieve success. Knowledge is a great addition to life, but it's the consistent practice and application of that knowledge that brings results and success; persistent practice is a theme that emerges throughout the book. To this end, in the final chapter, we will establish a DNA of Success blueprint in the form of a practical tool and give you your own framework that you can develop on your journey to success, as you see fit.

The DNA of Success has been a very remarkable journey for me personally and I have been privileged and proud to meet and work with some of the best individuals within the British and global business, political, art and charity communities not only in my career and personal relationships but also in the production of this book.

Ultimately, this book is about great stories, from great people who are willing to share both their great moments and some of their setbacks with us – my job has been to organise the principles of that achievement into a philosophy and a DNA of Success.

I trust that you will enjoy this book, and once you have read it I would welcome any insights and stories you may like to share from your successes.

Best wishes, **Chris Norton**
London, England **www.thednaof.com**

All successful people have been helped along the way by someone who believes in their potential. We can all instantly recall how we have benefited and learnt from others on our own success journey. We all need others to help us cultivate the 'golden seed' that is our true potential and this belief and value is far more powerfully linked to success than I could have imagined.

Without exception, when I asked our contributors: "Who helped you on your journey?", there was a clear, passionate and easily articulated identification of role models, key influencers, mentors and coaches as part of their success.

Equally, role-modelling and fast-tracking successes by learning from others are undeniably vital components for others to achieve success. Consequently, this chapter focuses on uncovering and exploring key elements around what is important in terms of success and how they have influenced our contributors.

Seven categories emerge within this key area:

- Letting great people shape our lives
- Having moral courage
- Achieving mastery
- Developing others
- Developing key relationships
- Seeking early leadership
- Having a visionary and futuristic outlook.

Letting great people shape our lives

I asked our contributors who were the key people in their success journey and what was inspirational and influential about them.

The concept of the big leader emerged strongly, as Penny Hughes explains: "Victor Blank was my chairman at Trinity Mirror and he was a really 'big leader' who gave me the confidence that I was operating on a level playing field."

Greg Dyke met John Cotter at Harvard Business School and talks about him as a key influence and role model: "He definitely influenced my life. He reinforced a belief I had that when you are running an organisation, it is all about the people. Your job is to make them feel good, feel valued and if you are doing that then you are doing it right. The importance of Cotter in my life was that he instilled confidence in me to keep doing this when you get into big organisations. I carried this with me to the BBC and my leadership was true to this value."

Graham Taylor highlights perhaps an unexpected key role model for leadership in Sir Elton John: "When I met Elton, at the time he interviewed me for the manager's job at Watford, I was really taken by his ambition, his huge goals and his absolute belief they were possible. His ambition was to take a struggling lower division team up to not just the Premiership but into European competition in five years. We achieved it. What I learnt was the power of setting long-term goals and also the art of being committed, keeping people accountable but not interfering. Elton was a great leader of the club in that era."

Frederick Forsyth cites Charles de Gaulle as having presence and leadership. "When I was in Paris in the 60s de Gaulle's presence, views and day to day thoughts captivated the lives of the French people. He was a leader in a true sense of touching all parts of French history and life at that time."

Alongside great leaders come great mentors. According to Hughes, Don Keough, the worldwide CEO of Coca-Cola, was one of these: "He made me the first female and the youngest vice president in the company at the age of 33. He had faith in me and he wanted to send a signal to the rest of the organisation that actually talent management can happen in a different way."

Another was Lord MacLaurin: "He was also a great mentor for me while I was at Vodafone. So, I would say that it is my mentors who have provided me with belief in myself to reach the goals I have achieved."

Baroness Dean's great mentor was Barbara Castle, who introduced the Equal Pay Act: "She gave me the opportunity to work at national level. She appointed me to the Supplementary Benefits Commission. She taught me how to use influence."

Vince Cable recalls how the late John Smith, the Labour Party leader, significantly helped him on his road to success in politics: "John was a politically strong, clever, human and generous man. He taught me how to operate as a minister, how to do politics; he was a major influence."

When it comes to role models and heroes, Sir Peter Squire's military career was inspired by Sir Basil Embry. Sir Peter cites reading his book *Wingless Victory* as a key determining factor in him deciding to join the Royal Air Force.

Forsyth, however, is not a hero worshipper and does not have role models. He believes that it is better to "admire than to hero worship".

In some cases, people may not be role models but can still influence our lives. According to Baroness Dean, Rupert Murdoch was not a traditional role model, but he was someone she respected very much at the time: "He was ruthless but focused on the main game and he was prepared to take a gamble."

People with a can-do attitude feature strongly. Both Forsyth and Hughes cite Margaret Thatcher as an excellent example of this. While Forsyth admires "her single-minded vision to overcome the bureaucrats in the Falklands campaign", Hughes, although not necessarily seeing her as a role model, could not "help but be influenced by her presence and the 'you can do it' attitude".

Another name that features in this category is Douglas Bader, who "was a man who overcame so much – had great tenacity," according to Forsyth.

So, a number of key lessons emerge:

- Role models are invaluable. Identifying the key values displayed by these people, and taking these values and attitudes into our lives where they feel congruent, fast-tracks success.

- Meeting and being involved with successful mentors takes us outside our experiences and boundaries. By doing this we get inspiration and application that we can take and replicate.
- It is possible to learn from people we do not necessarily consider role models. We may not admire all that they are or do, but they will have key attributes that can help us.

Finally, all of our contributors say that a mentor or coach must be someone we like, trust and admire.

The consistent view is that great value and momentum can be gained by letting great people shape our lives on the journey to success.

Having moral courage

Moral courage is a powerful learning theme mentioned many times by our contributors and is an absolute necessity for leadership and a key success driver.

Penny Hughes reflects on two key role models. The first is Sir Christopher Gent in his time as chief executive at Vodafone: "Vodafone became the largest telecoms provider in the world. The decisions he took along the way were bold. The way he put himself on the line was just incredible."

The second person she cites as having great courage of conviction is Dame Anita Roddick: "Her views around the environment and human rights were just fantastic. In particular she was world class in terms of understanding what a business needs to commit back to its community."

Sir Peter Squire is himself another inspiration in terms of the value of moral courage. The absolute belief in standing by tough decisions is a core value for Sir Peter in his life. He accepts that there may be times when these decisions are unpopular but as a leader these have to be made and followed through: "Clearly, there are times as a military force and as a commander where ultimately you have the final decision and you need to clearly communicate but as importantly stick by that decision. Through my career I have had to do this and I know it is a key value for a leader to aspire to and live by." As the book unfolds, there are some great examples of Sir Peter showing moral courage both in his personal decisions and as a leader.

Lord MacLaurin is a true 'role model' in relation to moral courage and his stand-off with Jack Cohen, so graphically described in his book *Tiger by the Tail*, shows real moral courage in fighting for the cause he believed in around a loyalty scheme for customers. In the face of massive opposition, he stuck to his beliefs and won through. This breakthrough is acknowledged as a key turning point in the success of Tesco.

Achieving mastery

Mastery of a specialist subject, area of business or skill comes through strongly as a lesson in learning from the best. Our contributors all focus on areas of mastery and specialism. They can adapt these in multiple roles and in different companies. However, they continue to develop their specialism throughout their lives and careers.

A graphic example of this is Frederick Forsyth, who still considers himself a journalist at heart. He strongly believes in the role of the investigative journalist in exposing corruption and the misuse of power and sees this as part of what makes the role feared by the establishment. He has taken these specialist skills and applied them to writing novels. This mastery has made him one of the world's leading authors for the past 40 years.

Penny Hughes has become, arguably, one of the most experienced specialist, non-executive directors and has been a board director for the past 15 years. She has held positions with companies such as Vodafone, Gap, Cable & Wireless and Reuters. Hughes sees her specialism as customers and employees in the retail, finance and technology sectors. Her career path began at a young age, in non-executive director terms, as she was only 36. This specialism was a definite choice for her and she is now a significant and sought-after presence in boardrooms worldwide. Hers is a graphic example of mastery and the attainment of excellence in a focused and repeatable area of expertise. She attributes this focused path to working with great people such as Don Keough of Coca-Cola, Sir Christopher Gent of Vodafone and Derek Williams of Cadbury Schweppes, among other mentors, supporters and role models.

Such is the emergence of mastery as a main constituent of success that we have devoted an entire chapter (Chapter 4) to this fascinating and vital area.

Developing others

Mentors have played a critical role in shaping and developing our contributors. They have:

- believed in their ability to succeed
- delegated responsibility to them
- had a powerful impact on them in terms of their values, beliefs and actions.

You will see multiple examples of these from both our contributors and the key influencers in their lives.

The key belief is that mentors are inspirational developers. They see potential in others – they are 'work in progress'. And, in turn, protégés are drawn to them, thus opening up the opportunity to experience success. There are many examples of this:

- Penny Hughes was given the opportunity to excel as the first woman vice president of Coca-Cola. She was also, interestingly, the youngest.
- Brenda Dean, through her mentor Joe Sheridan, was given the opportunity to be "a woman in a man's world" in reaching for the position of leader of a trade union – again, the first woman to do this.
- Graham Taylor was given a chance by a visionary chairman at Lincoln City as a young manager in his twenties in the "instant results business of soccer".

- Sir Peter Squire was given a command position in the world of the military during turbulent times of conflict in world history at the age of 27.
- Reuters showed enormous faith in Frederick Forsyth when he was sent to Paris at 23 to report on turbulent times in French history and Charles de Gaulle's presidency.

Our contributors have also taken on the role of mentor as part of their own beliefs and values, and continue to contribute to the success of others.

A perfect example of this is Lord MacLaurin. When asked about his greatest achievement at Tesco, he does not mention the phenomenal success the company enjoyed in his time as chairman, the global expansion, the customer loyalty or the number one position the company achieved in its marketplace. He considers his greatest achievement to be in succession planning, in particular his selection of Sir Terry Leahy for great things (and, interestingly, he also mentored Phil Clarke who has just taken over from Sir Terry). When Sir Terry Leahy stepped down from Tesco in June 2010, the stock market reacted to his departure with surprise and some £750m was wiped from Tesco's share price.

Developing key relationships

The fifth element of learning from the best involves two key relationships. The first comes in the form of an early life key influencer, while the second is a partner, wife or husband of at least 20 years' standing. These partners in success play a significant, acknowledged part of the success story.

The early life relationships are either parents or teachers who significantly influence the success blueprint. My first story is from Baroness Dean, who identifies her father as a role model and key influence in her early years: "Going back to my early days there is no doubt my main influence was my father – Hugh. My relationship with my father was very close. I guess most daughters say that but when he died, about four years ago, I became ill – it actually made me ill – something that has never happened to me before in my entire life. And I was ill for about six months, both emotionally and physically."

Hugh lived until he was 85 and he was an influence right the way through her life: "He was always there for me and as I got older and I got involved in trade unions, particularly in things like housing in pretty deprived areas, it made me realise just how important the family unit is to people, so I reckon I got a very good start in life."

Baroness Dean also has a brother who is 18 months younger than her. She describes her family as a very tight-knit unit: "Mother went out to work so I was a latchkey child. I was no doubt expected to go the 'wrong' way – to become a delinquent! I had the key on a piece of string round my neck so that my brother and I could get in."

So why was the relationship with her father so close? "Well, my father and mother were equal partners in bringing us up, which was most unusual at the time. It was not the norm in those days. They both worked shifts. Dad worked shifts on the railway so he was there two weeks out of three for my brother and me. When he was on the six till two shift, he would be there for us when we got back from school, and when he was on two till ten he gave us our breakfast, and indeed when he was on nights sometimes he would not go to bed until he had got us off to school. And he would cook our meals for us."

Baroness Dean believes that the relationship between her parents, though she did not think about it then, was really a very equal one for that time: "My father also fought for me to go to high school and to give me that chance. He was my hero. He taught me about equality and was a huge influence throughout my life."

She had another early key influencer – a teacher called George Booth: "He was a disciplinarian and everyone was frightened of him. Somehow I hit it off with him and he did everything for me and fought on my behalf to help me succeed at school. I learnt the joy of learning from him. I got the nickname 'Brenda Why' as I learnt the art of questioning from him."

Graham Taylor identifies his parents as having a unique impact on his life: "Dorothy, my mother, was a very positive person. She taught me that if you remain positive you retain control. If you are negative you give away your control. My mother was my first role model as a leader. She was the leader of the house in a loving but firm way, in terms of wanting the best for the family. She taught and showed me how to live with a 'never give up' attitude. It gave me ambition and commitment as key values."

Taylor's father, Tom, actively involved him in his work as a journalist: "He took me with him and it gave me a sense of pride and purpose to be involved. I had an idyllic childhood full of love and involvement and it was a great learning ground that gave me learning and foundations in what I needed for life and success." When Taylor had to resurrect his career after his setback with the England manager role, he drew on his early life and his parents' values and beliefs: "It was a huge part of getting me through."

Vince Cable's father also played a major role, but partly in a negative way. He was a strongly prejudiced man: "Through provoking me and through argument he got me interested in politics and political views. So he was important."

Greg Dyke recalls his father had a positive influence in terms of his great ability to talk to everyone and his belief that everyone had the right to be talked to: "This trait, I believe, I modelled in terms of the value of leadership through respect and contact with people."

Penny Hughes and Frederick Forsyth also trace back key values and beliefs to one of their parents. For Forsyth, it was his father who was "shrewd and wise". For Hughes, it was her mother's "great common sense and positive outlook on life".

So early life blueprints for success, especially from parents, come through strongly as a key contributor to success. This is not surprising, but what is remarkable is how these values show up time and time again, especially in times of difficulty.

The second key relationship is with long-term wives, husbands or partners. A partner is a great sounding board and a true strength in times of difficulty and setbacks. They are also detached enough to give real value in terms of clarity and input.

So for Taylor with Rita, Forsyth with Sandy, Hughes with David, Dyke with Sue, Baroness Dean with Keith, Sir Peter with Carolyn, and Cable with his first wife Olympia (who sadly lost her battle with cancer) and now his current wife Rachel, these relationships are a vital part in our contributors' success stories. This is true whether these relationships were formative or later in life and ongoing.

Seeking early leadership

Seeking early leadership is seen as a vital factor for success by our contributors, who all display a mindset of being the first. They have fast-tracked their success through high-profile, high-impact and high-achievement decisions.

Penny Hughes encapsulates this concept perfectly: "I have not set out to do this but I have specialised in being first."

Hughes was the first woman to be vice president of Coca-Cola and also the first person under 40. She was the first-ever non-executive director of Body Shop, which meant that when Anita Roddick tried to buy the business back she had to sit opposite her and represent the shareholders. Hughes was also the first non-Swede on the Swedish Bank board, which she describes as being "quite an experiment for them".

She was also the first non-US citizen to be on the Gap board, the first and only woman at that time on the Vodafone board, and the only woman on the Royal Bank of Scotland, Cable & Wireless Worldwide and Home Retail Group boards: "It gives me a different perspective and different values. Being the first has opened up so many opportunities for me and none I regret."

Looking for early leadership opportunities brings to life and creates opportunities for innovation. It speaks volumes about self-esteem and self-belief, and translates a vision for success into visible action. We cover these topics in more detail in Chapters 2 and 3.

Having a visionary and futuristic outlook

The seventh, and perhaps the most necessary and relevant, lesson from great people is around vision. Never has it been more important in times of ever-changing and turbulent political, cultural and organisational change to have the ability to envision, focus on and enable success in an inspirational way.

We could comfortably fill a number of books with views on how to do this, who has done this and what impact it has had on organisations and people. In terms of our DNA of Success and learning from the best, the key point emerging from this initial chapter is the need to recognise this ability in others, recognise the need to have it in ourselves and then take the opportunity to create the vision on our path to success.

What does a visionary and futuristic role model and leader look like? They are the kind of person who loves to peer over the horizon. The future fascinates them and they have the ability to see in detail what it might hold. This detailed picture keeps pulling them forward into tomorrow. While the exact content of the picture will depend on our other strengths and interests, be it a better product, a better team, a better life or a better world, it will always be inspirational to us.

People often look to leaders to describe a vision of the future. They want a picture that can raise their sights and their spirits, and great leaders can paint this picture for them. There is a quote from the American author Zig Ziglar, which takes this vision and starts to put it into practice: "I don't care how much power, brilliance or energy you have, if you don't harness it, focus it on a specific target and hold it there you are never going to accomplish as much as your ability warrants." Ziglar is describing what follows the vision, ie the need to set goals.

Some great leaders have acted as role models for our contributors and they read like a *Who's Who* of the past 50 years of influential people and business leaders, including Sir Elton John, Lord MacLaurin, Don Keough and Dame Anita Roddick.

We will cover more on each of these stories later, but the important point here is the need to access, mix with and learn from great visionaries as part of the inspiration, drive and enablement of our success.

Three key points clearly and consistently emerge:

1. Mentors, coaches, sponsors and a support network are key. They provide potential opportunities, inspiration and role-modelling that enable us to fast-track our success.
2. The key elements to focus on are goals and vision, mastery, moral courage and early exposure to and experience in leadership and innovation. The discovery of being the first within our contributors' DNA is a remarkable and worthy consideration.
3. Paying attention to relationships in early life and in our lifelong relationships, again, is a key part of any success story.

Sir Richard Branson, in his book *Business Stripped Bare: Adventures of a Global Entrepreneur*, says that it is important to surround ourselves with great people: "I surround myself with business coaches and mentors who act as sounding boards, helping to guide decisions. I also include reliable colleagues and co-workers who have similar goals, values and interests. These people naturally complement Virgin's ever-expanding cultural presence. Also, key to my belief in this area, I am surrounded by supportive family and friends who believe in me, my mission and vision."

Clearly, Sir Richard values having great people around him and it's clearly part of his value set.

Chapter 2 focuses on this topic, looking at our values and the value they bring to ourselves and others.

Chapter 2
Values and value

Values are a powerful determinant of human accomplishment, progress and fulfilment, and every individual has a core set of personal values.

Speaking to our contributors, I discovered an inspirational set of values and received a fascinating insight into these through the stories they told. Researching further, I discovered 690,000,000 entries on Google for the word 'values', so how could I gain a different perspective and achieve my goal in producing a DNA of Success around them?

I needed a way of producing a values 'blueprint of success' that went way beyond any simplistic view. To achieve this, I combined the interviews with some targeted research, my business experience, and a set of other inspirational value-based stories to produce a structure when looking at values as a contributor to success.

Additionally, I have extended the blueprint to include 'value', ie the contribution people make to other people, organisations and communities through their own personal values. For example, Baroness Dean is working with sixth form students, encouraging them to have more self-belief. This is about values in action producing success by application.

Particularly from my work in coaching in large organisations, I believe this extended definition will give us a key differentiator both when looking at our values and in producing our blueprint for success.

This chapter includes the following:

- An exploration of our contributors' key values and insights and how these are linked to success
- An inventory and practical framework for auditing and developing values – the aim is to develop a tool with six key value areas based on our contributors' top three values, the values I have uncovered in my research and those I see emerging in my day-to-day work coaching top organisations
- A section entitled 'It's the stories people tell about you'. This was the breakthrough for me and is inspired by a discovery I made in my interview with Greg Dyke. For me, this is a great example of how we

can live by our values, breathe life into our values and use our values to achieve success for ourselves and the people we work with and with whom we share relationships.

Our contributors' responses around values are very clear and very close to the DNA of how they live their lives and achieve their success. Seven key values emerge: self-belief, respect (for others), integrity, moral courage, tenacity and hard work, taking responsibility, and luck.

Self-belief

According to Greg Dyke, a positive mindset is key to success: "Knowing you will survive. The test is when times are tough and setbacks happen. Knowing you will get through it." He also takes this further into self-reliance and controlling our own destiny: "Take it. Nobody else will claim it for you."

His values are also allied to his beliefs around positive people: "Employ positive people. Help them, lead them, value them and they own the responsibility to be positive in their work. Employ them for their attitude and their skills."

For Sir Peter Squire, self-belief has played a key part in building his career: "I knew I wanted to progress and I always had the belief in myself that I would. When I joined the RAF, I did so because I wanted, first and foremost, to fly military aircraft. That was my over-riding passion but, at the same time, I knew that I also wanted to enjoy a full career and to do as well as I could in all aspects of the service. I never seriously thought about retirement even when the pyramid started to narrow."

Sir Peter was single-minded about flying, but also wanted to get on and progress. He knew as a flight lieutenant that he could make it as a squadron leader, then as a squadron commander and then as a station commander: "Of course, I was apprehensive at each promotion but, through watching others, I had the self-belief to tackle each new job with confidence. I believed in myself, knowing that I had the skills to succeed and I would have been disappointed if there had been a ceiling well below the top."

This illustrates the necessary self-belief that drives high self-esteem. In a military career, in order to succeed in a life or death moment, these values and living these values are crucial. However, they also transfer equally to us all.

For Baroness Dean, self-belief is a very personal value and one she finds lacking in other people, particularly young women. As part of her way of giving back to society, she visits sixth form schools to discuss her views on leadership and values.

Her advice is to be prepared: "Do your homework, study your brief, know your subject. If you don't, you will be found out and this will undermine your confidence. You have to put the work in to prepare. Then you will achieve and this will breed confidence as people will listen to you. People don't want to deal with unconfident people."

Baroness Dean believes that positive life experiences can be important, but you have to make them happen, go through them and build up your confidence.

Respect

For Penny Hughes, a key value is achieving balance in how she lives her life: being a good human being, enjoying life, showing respect for others, and balancing that with a sense of achievement and success.

Hughes's career is a blueprint of how to live this value. She was the youngest and the first woman vice president in Coca-Cola, at the age of 33. But in order to live according to her values, she left corporate life at 36 and took up a new career path as a non-executive director. While doing this she was bringing up her two children in what was then, for her, a fledgling career in this area. In Chapter 7 we cover how she 'chanced' upon her ideal role as an international non-executive director for Gap. This must have been, at the time, a risk in career terms but it was aligned to a strong value set around what she wanted in life. She believes in it passionately and she has made an outstanding success of it to the point where she is acknowledged as having had 15 years as one of the most experienced and respected non-executive directors in the UK. She has achieved this and lived her life through keeping her core values at the forefront of her mind.

Graham Taylor also believes that respect for people is extremely important, particularly in the context of team building: "To get the best out of people at all levels, it's about your ability to form and grow relationships, how to be successful together, as a team. It's the management of people to achieve the collective goal of success. You cannot be successful on your own. You are responsible for your own success but you need others to be with you."

Baroness Dean also believes in showing respect for the people you are dealing with: "My life was in some ways one long negotiation as a union official. However, whatever the outcome was, I always ensured that I would leave their dignity in place and I was always mindful of working at building respect in every interaction."

She was involved in the Wapping dispute of the mid-1980s, when two very powerful newspaper publishers, trade unions and the government were at 'war': "Once the dispute was over, it confirmed for me that you cannot achieve much by revolution in that situation and that to have any kind of bilateral relationship – whether it is supplier and customer or employer and trade union employee – whatever it is, there has to be respect. If you do not have respect for one another you are never going to achieve a good deal."

Once respect is lost at an organisational level it's very tough to win that back without some real shift in circumstances. At this point the relationship between the unions and the newspaper owners had gone: "The respect in Fleet Street between management and workers had been completely lost. In fact Rupert Murdoch said to me one day when we were trying to do a deal: 'The dance has changed but the music remains the same – I could do a deal with you Brenda, but what about your people?'"

Although Baroness Dean acknowledges that she respected Murdoch, the same cannot be said for Robert Maxwell – who ran the other half of the media establishment at the time – whom she did not trust. She explains: "It was not that I did not instinctively trust him, it was because of the experiences I had with him. For example, we would negotiate a deal and unless it was very complicated I very rarely asked for confirmation in writing. I would go and tell my members and then we would get it in writing afterwards. But with Maxwell, we would do a deal, I would tell the members and then he would renege on it. So with him I would not tell the members unless I had a piece of paper in my hand and then I would say: 'This is what he says and this is his signature. However, I cannot guarantee until you get your pay-packet what will be inside it if you accept this deal.'"

So there was a lack of respect and confidence in Maxwell, and Baroness Dean admits that she did not really like him either: "It was difficult to look him in the eye and have a conversation. Despite the fact that he was friendly and actually very good with women – respectful. He swore once at a meeting and had the decency to ring me the next day to apologise as his language had been appalling."

On one occasion there was a stoppage and the two unions and the industry went to court: "We got fined so there was a strike and our people were not going to go back to work until he [Maxwell] had paid the fine. He said he would. I asked him when he was going to pay it. My other colleagues were happy to accept that he would pay it. But the fine was actually on the unions so if it was not paid we would be in contempt and we would be fined even more. So he said: 'I will give you a cheque.' I replied: 'Actually, Mr Maxwell, may I suggest a bank transfer.' He was furious with me. I said: 'I do not want to impugn you but we do need to tell our members it has been paid.' And he did it. I did it quietly; I did not in any way insult him. However, without respect as a value that was the way I had to deal with him."

For Vince Cable, respect for others comes in the form of economic fairness: "There is a place for all to succeed in society. There should be fairness in the distribution of resources for all."

Integrity

Sir Peter Squire believes strongly in integrity: "It is about principles. Setting out what you believe in and sticking by that. I also believe you should never ask others to do what you are not prepared to do yourself."

Integrity is also one of Baroness Dean's top values. An example of this was during the Wapping dispute (see page 49). Throughout this, while fighting her cause and being acknowledged as a leader who made a difference within the union movement, she held on to her integrity: "My own personal values were really tested because there were occasions when I was asked to do things in my role as a union official that would have compromised my core values. So, putting up an argument you do not really believe in is easy and does not compromise your core values – but doing something that does compromise [them] is different."

For example, on one occasion there was some violence on the picket line and she was under a lot of pressure to condemn the police: "We had a very good relationship with the City of London Police but not such a good one with the Metropolitan Police. Leading them then was a guy called Rambo (who was subsequently sacked but not because of us). The Greenham Common protest was going on at the time and the women contacted us during Wapping to say we should beware of him. They said that he had a nice smile but he was not a nice person and not to be trusted."

When some union officials put her under pressure to condemn the police, her reply was: "What about the situation on Saturday night when rent a mob came along? What about the people who are not involved in our dispute but who have issues with the police?" (There were people from both the extreme right and the extreme left wings – the National Front and the Trotskyists.) So she decided to condemn violence on the picket line full stop, even though the officials did not want her to do this: "I said: 'This may seem a small issue to you but for me to compromise my integrity is a big deal.'"

And as far as Brenda Dean was concerned, as general secretary the members could have her time and her commitment, but not her integrity:

"Anything that would counter my integrity mattered, because once it is lost it has gone for ever. So you really do have to be true to yourself – and that is not being highfalutin or a goody-goody, it is about sleeping comfortably at night (although I admit having many a sleepless night during the dispute – but that was about delivering what I knew the members wanted and could I do it?). I knew that at the end of the dispute I wanted to still be Brenda Dean and not someone I did not recognise."

Moral courage

While Frederick Forsyth considers moral courage to be a key value, this is not the case for everyone: "Alas, often no morality exists, and it's not a requirement for success, as I've seen people at the top of their game who do not possess a single cell of this."

According to Sir Peter Squire, moral courage is needed in order to be able to take, and stand by, tough decisions: "There have been occasions when one has had to take really tough decisions and subsequently not necessarily be popular as a result. Clearly, as a military commander you have to do that but, equally, there are plenty of examples in all walks of life of similarly difficult decisions."

Penny Hughes provides an example of moral courage in business leader Sir Christopher Gent: "He was one of the very first employees at Vodafone, one of the largest telecoms providers in the world. The decisions he took along the way were bold and the way he put himself on the line was just incredible."

Vince Cable cites honesty as a key value and this is closely related to moral courage, as it is "being clear, straightforward and not 'dodging' the issue or question".

Tenacity and hard work

One of Penny Hughes's core values centres around a commitment to work. For her, it is the ability to focus, commit and know to put everything on one side and give 100% attention when it matters. She does this herself and expects the same from others. Throughout her time at Coca-Cola, she would, as she put it, "work hard and play hard" and instil that as a key organisational value.

Frederick Forsyth's views on tenacity are aligned to the values he lives by and also to how he sees these values in himself and others: "The first break alone is not enough, you need perseverance, and this is a very rare quality in my view." In Chapters 5 and 6, Forsyth's story about how he overcame both career and personal setbacks provides a graphic example of the value of 'tenacity' in action.

Vince Cable is also a great believer in hard word and tenacity: "You need to apply yourself to become a specialist and work at it repeatedly and with persistence and stamina."

Taking responsibility
In the world of sport, individuals are judged very publicly on their results. According to Graham Taylor, one's values are examined in the public domain even more intensely than in business. Because of the instant nature of sport and results, and the media coverage, one's values are often exposed to extremes of highs and lows and are extensively judged.

In both his personal and his vocational life, taking responsibility for results is a key value for Taylor: "As a manager you ultimately 'live and die' by these [results]. You are accountable. Your people have responsibility for their performance."

According to Taylor, parents 'frame' the values of their children and family, and "the same happens in the extended football family. Here the manager's values are constantly under scrutiny and the strength of these values determines how the team members' values are shaped and lived out."

Luck
Frederick Forsyth is a great believer in 'serendipity' and this aligns itself to a key factor in the DNA of Success: synchronicity, which is covered in Chapter 7: Synchronicity and Alignment. "You need to seize the luck," he says, "and have the acuteness to recognise when it comes along – *carpe diem*."

This section outlines an inventory and a practical framework for auditing and developing our values, the aim is to develop our awareness and application of them. This is at the heart of the 'DNA definition of values' and what they achieve.

The six values within our best practice framework are as follows:

- Authenticity
- Being the first
- Confidence
- Concern for others
- Continuous improvement
- The power of business values.

Authenticity
The first value within our framework is authenticity. What is authenticity? What emerges from my interviews is that the better we know ourselves, the better we can live and work with authenticity. For me, it is about people being true to their dreams and passions: doing what they really believe in and pursuing it with integrity. This shows to others the person's authenticity.

It's about the outward expression of truth formed from an inner knowledge, certainty and trust in ourselves. The question is: Are we being authentic? It has never been so important to earn the respect of others. It has never been so important to keep the promises we make to our colleagues and customers. And it has never been so essential to be authentic.

However, and herein lies the challenge, it has never been so hard to demonstrate authenticity, because of the social pressure to be like everyone else. The media, our peers and the world around us pound us relentlessly with messages designed to make us live by their values rather than our own. There's a huge pull to behave like the majority.

Sometimes in life we have to close our ears to the voices of others, and tune into our own voice. And that's what authenticity is all about:

- Feeling safe and comfortable in our own skin
- Learning to trust ourselves so that we work to our own values, express our own voice and be the best we can be
- Knowing who we are and what we stand for, and then having the courage to be ourselves in every situation, not just occasionally
- Being consistent and congruent, so that what we are on the inside is reflected by the way we play it out on the outside.

By being authentic and true to ourselves, we realise our true potential, achieve success and operate in a peak state more of the time.

The great American lecturer and poet Ralph Waldo Emerson summarised it well: "To be yourself in a world that is constantly trying to make you something else is the greatest accomplishment of all. Stay committed to your own purpose, vision, values and who and what you stand for as a person. When people doubt you, say you'll fail or suggest you're not good enough stand strong in your own skin and don't let them tear you down." In other words, there will never be a better you than you, or as Oscar Wilde put it: "be yourself ... everyone else is taken!"

We should ask ourselves the following questions:

- Am I being myself?
- Am I being authentic and the 'real deal' both personally and professionally?

Being the first
The second value to examine within our 'audit' is 'being the first'. Our contributors demonstrate this value by being pathfinders, innovators and actively seeking groundbreaking opportunities:

- Penny Hughes was the first woman vice president of Coca-Cola.
- Brenda Dean was the first woman to hold the position of leader of a trade union.

- Frederick Forsyth is the youngest-ever Royal Air Force pilot to get his wings on jets, at the age of 19.
- Graham Taylor became a manager in his mid-twenties.
- Greg Dyke pioneered the introduction of Freeview to the UK marketplace.
- Vince Cable is the first Business Minister in UK governmental history.

I conclude that all this is more than coincidental. Being the first means that you are innovative, can pursue a vision and do not fear taking a risk. You do not fear failure and you have high self-esteem.

Confidence

Our third focus is around the value of 'confidence'. I include this value as it is an outward sign of positive inward values and a mindset aligned closely to success. It's about high self-esteem, never being afraid to admit we are wrong or ask for help, and seeing no long-term downsides in doing this. It's about the development of confidence through continual practice and preparation. Always holding a 'winning self-image' is a strong predictor of success.

In my coaching sessions with clients, I am always amazed how once people achieve the breakthrough of truly believing in themselves, they can learn to live the value of 'never underestimating what already exists that makes them so special'. Confidence breeds confidence.

Concern for others

The fourth attribute within our framework for success is 'concern for others'. Our contributors are focused on a genuine concern and respect for others.

Sir Peter Squire goes to the heart of this value when talking about communication skills: "I enjoy talking to people at every level and I do not find it difficult, regardless of rank or status. It is all about getting the most out of people. You will get far more if they believe you understand and care, and are prepared to listen and empathise."

I conclude that perhaps the single most powerful way to succeed in life is to have more concern for our fellow human beings. Normally, we are overwhelmingly concerned about ourselves, driven by our own personal motives and ambitions. However, the happiest people lose themselves in the feelings, thoughts and aspirations of others.

I suggest a little experiment. When we meet with others, try putting ourselves in their shoes. Think only of what they want. Listen carefully to their thoughts and feelings, and show genuine concern and empathy. Do this for the entire meeting. Now watch how the interaction goes. Watch how the energy level of the other person increases. The other individual becomes more animated and involved. In addition, if we watch closely, we may notice some interesting things starting to happen. New ideas or fresh insights and perspectives may be revealed. Or a new interesting idea, project or event might suddenly come out of the discussion. This all happens because we have shifted our concern towards the other person.

Are we ready to 'forget ourselves' and be genuinely interested in the welfare of others? Are we willing to be tolerant and kind to others, listen attentively and silently to their words, be non-judgemental and open to their opinions and points of view? If we are, we're excellent candidates for great success in life, not to mention ever-increasing personal happiness and joy.

Continuous improvement
Our fifth, and one of the most interesting, values is the desire for continuous improvement. Both individuals and organisations can adopt this value. For example, continuous improvement for an individual might mean increasing their knowledge and skills in a particular area, a desire to improve their attitudes and temperament, or a desire to do things better or get the best out of things. A company, on the other hand, can implement the value by continually evaluating and upgrading its procedures, the way it interacts with its customers, the way it treats its employees and the way it interacts with its community.

In today's ever-changing world – with the demands of new technology, new applications and new skills putting more pressure on individuals – organisations need to perform faster and better. If we are not investing in our personal development and progression, we will be 'going backwards' and others and the pace of change will pass us by. We need to ask ourselves: What is our personal value in terms of continuous improvement?

A story to illustrate this comes from my time at Dell Computer Corporation. As a company, we had a focused value and belief about becoming number one in the computer industry. To turn this into practical steps, one of our goals was to do with continuous personal development. Although everybody wants to do it, various perceived constraints – around time, its value in the short term, and commitment – always come up. So we implemented a simple 'one hour a day' rule. The challenge was for everybody to find one hour a day to spend on their own development. This could be reading a book, writing a blog or listening to a personal development DVD. We created a massive momentum behind this and to this day I still stick to this philosophy myself, as do many of my colleagues. One hour a day equates to just over nine working weeks of training a year. This delivers real personal development and shows this value in action.

The power of business values
Our sixth auditable and key value set is within our business lives: the power of business values.

I am lucky in that I spend my working life with great organisations and in the company of individuals working in these great global businesses. Vodafone, BP, Skype and Dell, among them, afford me an invaluable insight into values within organisations. I have found six to be compelling when looking at successful organisations.

I have linked these to the key values of our contributors, as they also have operated within large corporate enterprises. So I believe that looking at values within a business context is a vital constituent of a successful blueprint. I have found that, for those of us who do have the power, authenticity and vision to truly change the values in our organisation, these six really resonate:

- **Continuous improvement** – the desire and ability of the company to develop and incorporate ways to improve itself.
- **Customer delight** – the positive emotional response and joy that the customer feels from interaction with the company's people, products and services. The most successful businesses have discovered a formula

that goes beyond product and service. Their business is providing delight to their customers by understanding their specific personal interests, anticipating their needs, exceeding their expectations, and making every moment and aspect of the relationship a pleasant or, better yet, an exhilarating experience.

- **Developing people** – the desire and ability of the company to improve the lot of the employees working for it. Businesses are most successful when the leaders are not merely concerned with their own interests (sales, profits, success) but also with the concerns of their customers, and even more so with those of their own employees. Total concern for employees brings the business to a state of unity, which can attract infinite accomplishment.
- **Innovation** – the desire and ability of the company to venture into new, breakthrough areas of opportunity.
- **Maximum utilisation of resources** – the desire and ability of the company to improve its performance by full utilisation of its current resources.
- **Commitment to society** – the commitment of the company to focus on the social needs and aspirations of society. Their greatest growth occurs at moments when companies align the development of these internal engines with the explosive emergence of new forces in society. Companies that can attune their business strategies to reflect the evolutionary change of society in several or all of their growth engines (market, products and services, organisation, people and finance) catch the growing swell of the wave of social advancement. Penny Hughes, in her position on the board at Body Shop, worked with Dame Anita Roddick, who truly believed in this value. They implemented it into their business strategy and lived it as part of their brand. They used unusual social and environmental campaigns extensively; the value of the involvement, synergy and commitment to society was part of the phenomenal success of this company.

So this framework with its six elements is designed to be a tool that stimulates our thinking around our values, how we value them and how we can bring them to life on a daily basis.

There are two key questions that we should continually ask ourselves about our values:

1.   What do I believe in and commit to?
2.   What have I put in place to achieve this?

It's the stories people tell about you

Finally, as I said at the beginning of this chapter, a real breakthrough for me as I was writing this book was in meeting Greg Dyke and hearing his value around 'it's the stories people tell about you'. By the time I met Dyke, I already had a well-developed blueprint established. However, his value set around people led me to include this element in my 'DNA blueprint' as an over-arching way of looking at values. Dyke's story relates to his time as Director General of the BBC.

"Within the creative business, if you walk into somewhere like a TV company and they think you only care about money, you are 'finished' as a leader," says Dyke. "Most of the people are there because they care passionately about what they do, and you have to care passionately about that too. If you don't, you have not got any credibility. So when I joined the BBC, I came up with the line (I pinched the idea from Bill Clinton's line 'It's the economy stupid') 'It's about the programme stupid'. Only the programmes matter."

When he joined the BBC, Dyke started talking to everyone: "They were not used to it. In bigger organisations where you cannot get to know everyone, it is all about the stories they tell about you. So if you walk into the office and don't say 'hello' to the receptionist, or you don't shake hands with the security man, or you wander around with a 'grumpy face', that is what they will say about you. So if your stories are positive and you are true to decent values around people, that's as good as it gets. If you have done that, it means that in difficult times they will trust you."

There is an interesting footnote to this story: when Dyke resigned from the BBC in 2004, there were mass walkouts from the staff in his support, and over 800 people protested at his resignation and the circumstances surrounding it, which is a true test that he 'walked the walk and talked the talk' in terms of this value around people.

This story is a great summary piece to conclude our journey around values: treating people with respect; seeing trust as a key value in people and in organisations; making our values valuable to ourselves and those we live and work with; and inspiring people to believe in us.

We all need to look at the stories people tell about us, our leadership and our values. If we aren't aware of our values, don't live our values – and the people we deal with on a day-to-day basis don't believe in us – we have no basis for the creation of 'followship', which is our topic in Chapter 3.

One of the elements that has made our contributors successful is 'followship': instead of relying on the hierarchical structures that are typical in many organisations, leaders create teams and communities through consensus and inspiration, thus creating followers. My definition is based on my experience of seeing great leaders in action through my work in global corporate companies. Our contributors all demonstrate leadership by inspiration rather than by coercion.

Seven key themes of leadership

My focus in this book is on the DNA of Success. I want to show the DNA of leadership in real-life situations and to give it a practical orientation. My framework consists of three main topics:

1. **Emotional connection/intelligence** – how we manage our emotions and those of other people. It's about understanding and self-awareness, personal goals, intentions, responses and behaviours. It is then about replicating these in our understanding of others. When we get it right, it creates an emotional connection that builds trust and relationships with people. The breakthrough in this area came in a book by Daniel Goleman, a writer and lecturer on psychology and leadership, called *Emotional Intelligence* (1995). His work gave the concept of EQ (emotional quotient) a place in personal development and in the business world.

2. **Practical intelligence** – the way we work with people; how we think and act when dealing with people and situations. This is the practical output of our emotional intelligence and IQ (intelligence quotient), as I explain below.

3. **Five positive success traits** – which appear consistently in the success stories, actions and mindsets of our contributors and are supported and verified by my subsequent research:

   - Confidence
   - Tolerance
   - Empathy

- Positivity
- Respect for others.

Together, I call these points the 'seven key themes of leadership'. In this chapter, I will:

- explain the leadership intelligence model and its relevance to this subject area
- expand on each of the seven key themes of leadership – uncovering the key elements and substance within them – in order to construct a robust, practical and applicable set of knowledge, skills and behaviours
- develop and embed the five success traits into a practical leadership model, which will provide not only a blueprint and framework for this subject but also a 'mental model' for application in any other key areas in which you want to carry out a personal development study. This tool is used extensively and successfully in coaching, training and development and also in the field of personal development globally. I offer it as a resource for your consideration and use.

These three areas will provide a foundation block of mindsets, toolsets and skill sets for application in the creation of 'followship', which is a key foundation principle and enabler within our DNA of Success blueprint.

The leadership intelligence model

One of the breakthroughs in my coaching business has been the discovery, through my connection with Mahan Khalsa of Ninety Five 5, of a model relating to 'intelligence'. I have expanded the model and made it relevant and applicable to the DNA of Success. However, part of its value is its application to multiple areas of personal development. In this chapter, I use it to simplify, clarify and amplify the key principles of leadership and the creation of followship.

Intelligence is often a difficult concept to capture, and it is even more difficult for people to see how to progress and to make sense of strengths and weaknesses/development needs in this area. The purpose of the model described below is to demystify this. The model looks at three forms of intelligence as a methodology for real, in-depth understanding of any area. This works particularly well where some of the topics are soft skills, behaviours or concepts. It allows clarity and ensures that total understanding is possible. This can be at an organisational, subject, process or skill level.

The three intelligences we are going to use for our DNA topic of leadership and creation of followship are described below:

- **EQ – emotional intelligence (quotient)** – our emotional intelligence, or EQ, is about 'personality' attributes such as self-awareness, managing emotions and the connection to others through motivation and empathy. It's about our relationships and ability to communicate with others to establish a connection. As mentioned earlier in this chapter, Daniel Goleman was the driving force behind this concept.

- **IQ – intelligence (quotient)** – our intelligence, or IQ, covers the breadth and depth of our knowledge. It includes both our innate and our acquired knowledge (through education). However, it goes way beyond these to include our specialist knowledge and all areas of knowledge that can be learnt and developed.

- **PQ – practical intelligence (quotient)** – our practical intelligence, or PQ, is about the way we take our EQ and IQ into situations and how we work and think through life. It covers areas such as clarity of communication, critical analysis of situations and people, our quickness of mind and problem-solving abilities.

Leadership intelligence (quotient) is the sum of these three intelligences, so **LQ** = IQ + EQ + PQ. As we develop our mindsets, skill sets, knowledge and experience of each area of intelligence, our overall leadership intelligence will grow.

The DNA Of Success Leadership Intelligence Model

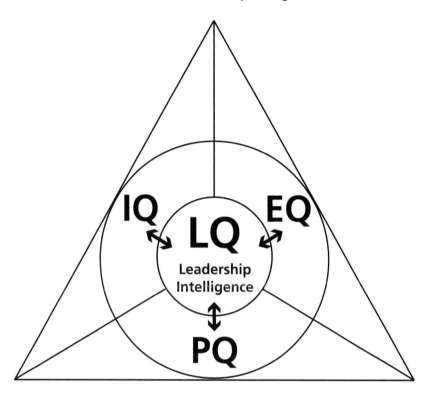

This model enables us to audit where we are in each intelligence area and can be used as a development tool to help in our continuous improvement.

Below, we expand on each of the seven key themes of leadership and at the end of the chapter we will populate the model to give us a DNA of Success structure for creating followship enabled by leadership intelligence.

Emotional connection/intelligence

From my research and interviews, it is very clear that our ability to make a connection emotionally with others is key to success. This is also underpinned by the work of Goleman (mentioned above). I would like to use an example from my coaching practice to bring this topic to life:

> Imagine yourself at a music festival, sitting on the grass and listening to and enjoying the great music and experience of the festival. Your favourite band or song comes on and you are so moved that you get up and start to dance. There are ten thousand other people sitting and just watching you but you are unaware of their attention, laughter and conversations about what you are doing. You are enjoying yourself, lost in the moment and totally in tune with the music. Suddenly, another person gets up and starts to dance with you. You acknowledge them and include them in your dance routine. Now two more get up and join in. Suddenly, the movement is growing and 20 more have joined in – now that's fun. People seem to have forgotten any risks. Those not taking part look uncomfortable as the masses join in. You have created a following.

For those of you who have not seen this, have a look at YouTube and search 'Sasquatch music festival 2009 guy starts dance party' – it's fun and insightful. So, what are the messages for creating a movement or followship?

- The dancing guy is the leader. He has total belief in his outcome and is prepared to stand alone with self-belief and self-confidence.
- He gets his first follower. He nurtures them, as they are an important statement, and treats them as an equal.
- He makes it easy to follow, so more people quickly join the movement.
- While the first guy gets the credit, it's the first person to join who transforms the leader from being on his own to having a 'following' that believes in him.
- There is no movement without the first follower. We are ineffective unless we create followship.

I was working in a coaching session with a talented product engineer who was a great innovator. His product was excellently designed and the market potential was phenomenal. However, in his company he could not get support, finance or capture the imagination of the key sponsors he needed. He quickly worked out in the coaching session that he needed followship, not more product enhancements or more financial plans. We created a set of events to attract and capture the first follower. Within a matter of weeks he had the largest community following him on social media in the company. He had his finance and he had his momentum and tipping point. What he did was create a movement of belief and trust and a group of advocates and followers.

We have already seen in Chapters 1 and 2 how our contributors have used and embraced 'being the first' as a success factor. Initially they were the followers of key mentors such as Don Keough at Coca-Cola, who had the faith to give Penny Hughes the role of vice president at the age of 33. He wanted to create a movement to bring forth a new dimension to talent management. Each of our other contributors has a 'being the first' profile. Their stories have emerged and will continue to emerge as the book progresses.

From my research, input from our contributors, Goleman's work on EQ, and my own experience from my coaching practice, I have identified four areas of EQ that are relevant and practical for our DNA project:

- Self-awareness
- Self-management
- Social awareness
- Emotional skills.

These areas are developed in the table over the page.

Emotional intelligence – the 20 key areas of focus

Self-awareness	Self-management	Social awareness	Emotional skills
Emotional self-awareness: The ability to read and understand our emotions as well as recognise their impact on work performance, relationships and the like	**Self-control:** The ability to keep disruptive emotions and impulses under control	**Empathy:** Skill at sensing other people's emotions, understanding their perspective and taking an active interest in their concerns (one of the five key behaviours in this chapter)	**Visionary leadership:** Inspiration of ourselves and others through a compelling motivational vision
Accurate self-assessment: A realistic evaluation of our strengths and limitations	**Trustworthiness:** A consistent display of honesty and integrity	**Organisational awareness:** The ability to navigate corporate life, networks and politics	**Communication:** Listening and clear, convincing and relevant messaging to people we are working with
Self-confidence: A strong and positive sense of self-worth and self-esteem (one of the five key behaviours in this chapter)	**Conscientiousness:** The ability to manage ourselves and our responsibilities	**Customer savvy:** Recognising and meeting customer and client needs	**Negotiation and influencing:** Having a toolbox of persuasive tactics
	Adaptability: Skill at adjusting to changing situations and overcoming obstacles	**Community contribution:** Looking to play a part in the bigger picture within our community	**Developing others:** Inspiring performance in others through coaching guidance and feedback
	Achievement orientation: The drive to meet an internal standard of excellence		**Conflict management:** The ability to manage disagreements to resolution
	Initiative: A readiness to seize opportunities		**Building relationships:** The ability to build and maintain a wide network
			Team working: A competence in co-operation and teambuilding

This inventory, of which two key elements – confidence and empathy – are covered below in more depth, gives a great insight and starts to demystify EQ and how to focus on these capabilities.

One element from the EQ skills area that is worthy of more detail at this point is visionary leadership. This first emerged in Chapter 1, when our contributors discussed their own mentors' key traits. As our contributors have repeatedly demonstrated a visionary approach in their careers, this element is worthy of deeper exploration.

A key and consistent theme around creating followship is that leaders must be believable and congruent in the way they lead their lives; they must be transparent and unafraid to show blind spots or areas in need of self-development. Followers will be inspired and have faith when they see a leader who is believable. Good leaders have confidence and the courage to act on intuition. Timing and experience are key in decision making.

Before moving on from visionary leadership, it is worth mentioning Robert Holden, PhD, and his book *Success Intelligence*, which captures a key point about authentic leadership. Holden is a gifted author and an excellent life coach who works in some leading global organisations. His work as director of the Happiness Project has been featured on *Oprah, Good Morning America* and two BBC television documentaries.

He outlines his view on what he terms the self-principle, and his insight into leadership and success is uniquely different. This principle, he believes, is the essential key to potential and talent, transformation and growth, success and happiness. He states unequivocally: "The quality of your relationship with yourself determines the quality of your relationship with success, happiness, love, god, money, time, health, luck and everything."

How does he believe this works? He sees self-knowledge as a good starting point: it is our central reference system for every other type of intelligence or wisdom. The better we know ourselves, the better we can live and work with authenticity and authority. Self-knowledge helps discern between true purpose and pointless goals. It teaches us about inner strength and true values. The more we know ourselves and are self-accepting, the more we can trust our wisdom and liberate our talent.

I have included Holden's views on the self-principle and self-awareness, as I believe they talk directly to our DNA leadership model, which provides a means to audit and develop our self-awareness within three key intelligence areas.

Practical intelligence

Practical intelligence is not just IQ. In DNA of Success terms, it's about how to interact with people and situations. Our contributors all demonstrate five areas of expertise, 'tools in the box' that come up time and time again as components of success with people, situations and within their core values and beliefs:

- **Heightened awareness** – awareness of our environment, following our instincts and initiating, being good observers of people, the art of being observant.
- **Healthy scepticism** – not being cynical, but being good evaluators of people and situations, noticing and reading the subtle clues.
- **Resourcefulness and flexibility** – being creative and having the ability to do extraordinary things when needed, persisting until we succeed (see Chapter 5), looking for the solution instead of focusing on the problem, being flexible in our approach to people, adapting to their preferred style of communication and personality.
- **Reasonable risk taking** – balancing planning/contingency with a drive to move to action. Our contributors showed great planning abilities and ability to review risks. However the over-riding mindset was to move to action.
- **Focused on outcomes** – avoiding procrastination. In his book *Think and Grow Rich*, Napoleon Hill analyses several hundred people who have accumulated serious wealth and success, and concludes that every single one of them reached decisions promptly. He contrasts this with those he interviewed and analysed who had been less successful, in his measurement system, around money. Those who fell into this category reached decisions very slowly, if at all.

On this last point, decision making, all our contributors show great strength, including focusing on results and following through rigorously with their own actions and the actions of others. This reminds me of the

Jack Welch quote taken from his book *Jack: Straight from the Gut*: "I'm always looking to create opportunities for success and I am always looking to remove any grey areas around accountability." Our contributors show complete synergy with this concept in applying it to themselves and others.

The five positive success traits

Confidence
Our contributors demonstrate three key factors in developing confidence, all from 'within themselves':

- Believe in yourself.
- Trust your own judgement and subsequent intuitive messages.
- Trust your own resourcefulness.

The combination of these three beliefs can be thought of as self-esteem (SE). They relate to self-image (SI) and self-confidence (SC): in mathematical terms, $SE = SI + SC$.

As can be seen in Chapter 6, self-confidence has enabled our contributors to operate, survive and thrive in a world where failure happens. Overcoming setbacks and having the ability to come through them is a direct result of self-esteem. Confidence grows through 'victories' and 'accomplishments', each one giving more self-confidence and an increase in self-image, and subsequently driving self-esteem upwards.

Confidence is also 'viral'; it is contagious and spreads. People are drawn to and inspired by confident people. As part of our DNA of Success, confidence is a key prerequisite for creation of followers and for leadership.

Tolerance
Tolerance manifests itself as an openness to accepting opinions and practices that are not our own. It is often a blueprint formed in our early years. It's either nurtured by our parents and role models, or ignored or 'driven underground'. This is a key attribute, as without the ability to change one's mind, accept input and be inclusive of others, followship is impaired or disabled entirely.

This quote from Harry S. Truman captures the essence of creating followship through this 'skill': "You can accomplish anything in life, provided that you do not mind who gets the credit."

Empathy ('connection')

The root of the word 'empathy' derives from the Greek 'pathos', which means 'feeling'. It's about connecting with people at their level of feeling. All our contributors are 'comfortable with themselves' and their own feelings. Empathy with others is authentic when empathy exists within ourselves.

Positivity

Our contributors exude positive energy, which is proven as both a value and a contributor to successful outcomes. I define it as 'mastering a state of mind' where we have a positive expectation of people and situations. In his book *The Power of Positive Thinking*, Dr Norman Vincent Peale sums it up as follows: "It's one universal truth that the attitude we hold helps shape the reality we experience."

Maintaining a positive attitude comes from inside ourselves and has to be part of our core values and belief system. Without this strong internal referencing, our positivity will always be knocked by negative opinions and negative people, and will not survive the setbacks that inevitably happen in life. I refer to this in my coaching as having "success" consciousness rather than "fear consciousness". This reinforces my belief that positivity is a state of mind that can be developed and is a "habit" exuded by successful people.

Respect for others

Respect for others shows itself not only in what people say but also in what they do. This is a dominant 'driver and value' for our contributors.

Greg Dyke sums this up when talking about the creation of followship: "It's not about 'them' vs. 'us', you need to focus on meeting their needs and yours. Do unto others as they would like done to themselves. If you treat people with respect they will believe in you."

I have populated the creation of a followship intelligence model with a cross-section of the intelligence skills we have uncovered in this chapter. This gives a practical framework for looking at our own development, in terms of both our strengths and areas of potential.

The Leadership Success Intelligence Model

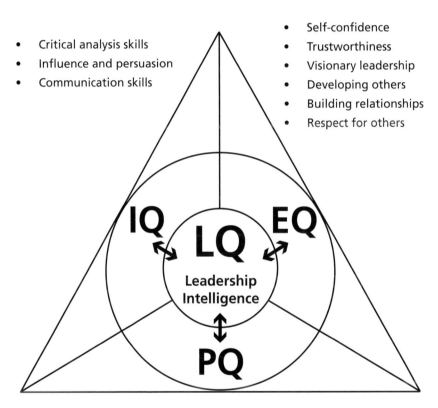

- Critical analysis skills
- Influence and persuasion
- Communication skills

- Self-confidence
- Trustworthiness
- Visionary leadership
- Developing others
- Building relationships
- Respect for others

- Adaptability
- Initiative
- Achievement orientation
- Positiveness

Chapter 4 offers another potential use of the tool, as we cover mastery and its role in the DNA of Success.

Chapter 4
Mastery

Mastery is a key part of the DNA of Success. There are three elements to mastery: general knowledge, innate talent and experience. While all three elements are valid in themselves, each on its own is not a sign of mastery.

General knowledge, often referred to as 'IQ', is the most widely recognised of these three elements and the one that is most prevalent in our lives: knowledge is gathered through school, university and continued learning and development. But knowledge itself is only a potential power in mastery. It is how we develop, apply and sustain it that makes the difference, turning it into a real power that delivers success.

There is a belief that people are born with an innate talent and that this equates to mastery. However, the gifts possessed by the best performers are not at all what we think they are. Some researchers now argue that specifically targeted innate talents are simply fiction. According to Geoff Colvin, senior editor-at-large for *Fortune*, in his book *Talent is Overrated: What Really Separates World-Class Performers from Everybody Else*, we are not naturally born concert pianists, car salespeople or brain surgeons. No one is. This theme will be explored further in this chapter.

The third element is what I term the 'experience trap', which is the belief that if we possess enough experience in life or in a role, we are a master. We all have examples in our personal and business lives that disprove this: the person with the most experience is regarded as the expert, but this is not translated into success either career-wise, or through a task or key goal. Research highlighted in Colvin's book shows that people can actually get worse with experience. In one case study covered in Colvin's book, experienced doctors actually scored lower on tests of medical knowledge than less-experienced doctors. Hence doctors are now encouraged to take refresher courses throughout their careers.

However, what really creates mastery is when we add in passion, drive and deliberate practice. Below, we look at seven key topics around the learning and acquisition of mastery:

- Deliberate practice
- Developed talent

- The role of the coach/mentor
- Mental models
- Passion and drive around innovation
- Investing in learning
- The application of mastery.

The first is deliberate practice. The key to sustainable success lies in the principle of constant and deliberate practice and it is absolutely ingrained in our contributors' success DNA. Based on my interviews, research and on further work with Mahan Khalsa, I believe that deliberate practice can be divided into seven components:

- Defined elements
- Repetition
- Feedback loop
- Mentally demanding
- Continuous improvement
- Passion and drive
- A lifetime of mastery.

Defined elements

It is necessary to focus on sharply defined elements of performance that need to be learnt or improved upon. Deliberate practice is when we define, identify and practise these elements; this period can be termed the 'learning zone'.

Lord MacLaurin from his early time at Tesco focused on and became a master innovator around consumer loyalty. His introduction of the loyalty card into Tesco was the first big push into consumer loyalty in retail. Lord MacLaurin has continued to evolve this area of mastery throughout his tenure as the head of both Tesco and Vodafone and he has taken this area of mastery with him through his 50 years of business experience and success.

Repetition

High repetition is the most important difference between practice and the task or game for real.

Greg Dyke says that he is a broadcaster at heart. He keeps this specialisation alive through his continued involvement and interest in the broadcasting industry, and no doubt we may see him emerge again within this arena.

Feedback loop

Feedback on results is constantly available; a teacher, mentor or coach is vital for this feedback loop.

Graham Taylor has held every position within football from player to coach to international manager and chairman. However, his roots and upbringing had brought him into the world of journalism through his father. Taylor has always valued the skills of journalism and has kept his knowledge and ability to commentate on the game alive throughout his career. This mastery allowed him to step straight into prestigious roles in radio, TV and the media when he finished managing at the highest level.

Mentally demanding

Mentally, it's demanding. It's about focus and concentration. Deliberate practice takes great performers past what others think of as limitations.

Penny Hughes is a non-executive director extraordinaire specialising in retail, finance and technology sectors. Talking to her, it became apparent that following her meteoric rise within Coca-Cola, she needed to think through how she was going to balance her life at the time. She had two young children, a husband and a career, and she wanted to be able to enjoy a work–life balance and at the same time use her extensive experience and achievements at that point. So she targeted her speciality at becoming a highly engaged and effective non-executive director and now, 16 years on, she has turned that into mastery.

Hughes explains: "I find myself at 52 and I think that I am probably among the most experienced non-executive directors in the country. I have held four or five positions over 15 years, which means I have done about 70 annual cycles of being on a board – 70 AGMs, 70 annual business plans, 70 of this, that and the other – and this is effectively a lifetime. And yet I think I have at least another 10 years to go. While I am experienced now and a specialist, I continually have to keep my focus on new emerging trends and market changes; this keeps my specialism current."

Continuous improvement

It is important to focus on what we are not yet good at and to practise this until we are good at it. Great performers never allow themselves to reach the 'automatic, arrested-development stage' in their chosen field. They avoid falling into automatic mode and they are always seeking to be better. This is a key difference between masters and non-masters – non-masters allow themselves to see or experience a 'ceiling'; masters push through this barrier and have a continuous improvement mindset.

Vince Cable became the voice of financial reason during the recent global economic crisis of 2008; he talked in everyday language with credibility, authenticity and simplicity, and he reduced complex global issues to everyday language to which people could relate. The point here is that Cable kept his financial speciality up to date and relevant although he had moved from his financial position in Shell to a career in politics, where at the time he was not necessarily required to have that financial expertise.

"People need to develop a few, but not too many, specialist areas of competence where they become crucially important as they know as much as anyone else," says Cable. "One of the dangers of being in politics is that a lot of people know a little about a lot – that is fine, but there have to be one or two areas where you have such a command that people treat you with respect and come to you for comment or advice. So you have to invest in acquiring real knowledge and expertise in certain areas."

Passion and drive

True passion can be driven by both internal motivators (the will to succeed or the motivation to overcome something) and by external factors (outside influences and circumstances). Often the two co-exist and fuse into a powerful force. What is undeniable, however, is that without the internal motivators nothing happens in terms of mastery and its continuation.

Frederick Forsyth is one of the most globally prolific authors of our time. His roots started in journalism and when I talked to him it was clear that he still considers himself a journalist at heart and still has a passion and drive to continue his journalistic skills and use them within his career as a novelist. "My background is that of an investigative journalist and my application of this competence is to tell stories, and I have been doing this since I was 31 years of age. In truth I didn't know I had it; it emerged accidentally," he says.

An investigative journalist's job is to be curious and sceptical, to keep asking the 'how' and the 'why' questions. Forsyth explains: "We should also be able to expose and ensure that people in power are held accountable. If you do not possess these characteristics or are unwilling to use them, you will simply be a commentator. A great example of this in action was Watergate. I've continued throughout my life to try to build on my background which was originally centred around journalism and then to use this in my career of writing novels."

A lifetime of mastery

Research shows that even masters suffer the inevitable decline in cognitive abilities, speed and memory power. However, masters keep performing at a high level even while their skills outside their specialist domain have deteriorated. The difference is continued, repeated practice. Through neuro-science we now know that our brains have the ability to add new neurons and form pathways well into old age when conditions demand it.

Baroness Dean started her mastery programme in her mid-twenties from a relatively humble background and has continued to develop her specialism even into her sixties, although the area in which she applies her mastery has changed. From being a trade union activist dealing with significant forces in the print arena, such as Robert Maxwell and Rupert Murdoch, she moved into the realms of UK government and UK business. However, the mastery of chairmanship through "elegant powerful negotiations" has been her area of focus and mastery throughout this 45-year period.

So the clear message that emerges is the importance of defining an area of specialism: ensure that it is an area of great passion and continue to develop this in order to be known as the master.

As discussed at the beginning of this chapter, the concept of specific innate talents may simply be fiction and we may not be born with a natural talent. However, our contributors demonstrated talent early in their lives and careers and continue to develop and hold onto it as a core competency irrespective of changing roles, changing life focus or changing career direction.

Baroness Dean, through her dealings with the trade unions and in particular Robert Maxwell and Rupert Murdoch, became a master negotiator. She then adapted this to become a master chairman.

She says that, without realising it, her trade union experiences trained her to become a chairman: "You do not just listen to what people have to say, you watch their body language and you try to make sure that everyone who wants to have a say gets one and that they 'own' the decisions that are made at that meeting."

"I enjoy chairing meetings," she continues. "You do not let people waffle on and on. Sometimes you will go to a meeting and someone will think they can keep popping in as if it is a conversation. It is not – it is about doing business. The trade union movement was very strict on that. In a formal debate you could only speak once. You cannot come back in, so you say all you need to say once. Many of the debates were timed so you could not waffle on. That sort of discipline was invaluable."

According to Baroness Dean, when trade unionists come to the House of Lords they find it easy to debate whereas many business people do not as they have not had the discipline: "I have been in meetings with really successful businessmen who have no idea how to chair a meeting. They let people go on and on. So chairing a meeting is a skill."

She also believes that it is necessary to draw out opinions from those who are not natural speakers, but who may well have something very valuable to add to the debate. This you can also observe from body language:

"Often these people, if not given the chance to air an opinion, will not object to the decision but after the meeting they will often vent some form of dissatisfaction. And sometimes you have to impress upon them that there are two remaining important items to get through and time is of the essence. At Covent Garden we would often have to look at things again. I would say: 'We are having a sweeping out all corners discussion.' None of it will be recorded but I wanted people to tell me totally honestly how they feel about things."

When Baroness Dean was at the Armed Forces' Pay Review Body, they were setting the pay increases for our armed forces and had quite a mix of people from business, trade unions, academia, etc. She explains: "I would try to find out what they thought was the right level to pitch the pay awards and this was obviously very difficult. The trade unionist would go 3% above everyone else, the businessman would be far lower and I had the officials who needed somewhere to start for the financial modelling on what it would cost."

She devised a system whereby she would say: "In today's meeting we are going to have a discussion which is a top of the head discussion about where we fix this pay award – BUT after this discussion you are all going to forget what you have said and you are not going to be held to that figure at all. If you want to turn it upside down you can – it is just so that we can get a feel and when you come next time we get a result."

So it would be structured as having two discussions on the subject: "Some people were not sure but, as I said, at the end of the day everyone had to buy into it so we would have this wonderful, free discussion where anyone could say anything. For example one would say let's go for 8% and I would say, 'Where is the money coming from?' At the end I would say 'thanks' to everyone and 'forget what we have said'. But then I would sit back and assess where we could find a range – a ballpark figure so that when we returned the following week there was somewhere to start."

According to Baroness Dean, a chairman must never say to a board "Take it or leave it," because that route will not lead to a true board decision:

"They will say later on that they were not happy about it – ie it was pushed through. So I have a personal policy wherever I am, that for any important decisions we have two discussions. At the first meeting the management can float what they are thinking of doing; then we pull out the 'grot' in them and see what we can do with it. Then we take it back the next time and in the interim they have had time to talk about everything so that when you arrive at the actual decision at least the majority are hopefully with you. People who go into a meeting where there are really important decisions to make are right to want to have time. You might put a paper round before the meeting saying 'have a read', 'give me a call', whatever. Quite often board members will talk to the CEO rather than me, which is good. And the foundation of all this came from my union days." Baroness Dean is a perfect example of developed talent and this DNA of Success component applied.

The role of the coach/mentor

Our contributors identify the role of mentors and coaches as a key success factor in their early lives and throughout their careers. In Chapter 1 we covered learning from the best, where a key element of success is role-modelling relevant people in our lives. The coach/mentor principle takes this to a new level in terms of having somebody who can significantly add to our expertise and learning as a coach and guide to help drive our mastery.

Penny Hughes says that without the support of the likes of Sir Christopher Gent, Lord MacLaurin and Sir Victor Blank she would never have achieved her success: "My mentors provided me with the belief in myself to reach the goals I have achieved."

Mental models

A mental model forms the framework on which we hang our growing knowledge of our speciality. New information is added to what we already know and builds up our bank of expertise. When interviewing our contributors, I found that they have a very fast and effective way of articulating and describing their key skills and reducing the complex to the understandable. This intrigued me and I was then able to correlate this skill to the way they operate within their key areas of mastery.

What distinguishes our contributors and led me to research this area was their ability to hold very complex sets of information but then be able to articulate them rapidly and comprehensively with clarity. In researching this, through the work of Richard Shiftman, published as a series of memory studies between 1968 and1997, I found that the average short-term memory only holds about seven items. Everybody's short-term memory falls into the range of five to nine items. What I found was that great performers use the same '5–9 chunks', but each chunk contains more information, so what in fact is happening is that great performers build mental models within a framework of short-term memory, but this is then much deeper in terms of what each element of short-term memory holds. This framework allows us to have complex topics available to articulate easily and effortlessly.

Baroness Dean provides an example of this. When we discussed her speciality around negotiations, it emerged that she has a mental model of how she has developed this from what began as expert negotiation skills learnt when making her way to the top of the trade unions as the first woman president of SOGAT. She then applied this skill set in governmental and corporate life when she moved from the unions into the House of Lords. Her specialism developed into mastery as a very successful committee chairman. I use the word 'chairman' deliberately, as she stresses the complete lack of the need to be referred to as a 'chairperson' – this is part of her strategy of success that we touch on in Chapter 6.

Baroness Dean has a three-part model that she can build on extensively and apply. The three elements of the mental model are:

1. Building trust through understanding the other person's point of view
2. Establishing a potential point of agreement early
3. Seeking always to identify and gain consensus by all stakeholders.

Baroness Dean can apply her mental model and extend it to new and complex areas; she can adapt and be adaptable, as she can build from her base level of knowledge and expertise. This is a great example of using mental models.

An example is the 'Freedom to Fly' campaign – a situation many believed was irresolvable – about the future of the UK airports and the UK aviation policy in the early 1990s. The government's view was that they must push ahead with expansion plans if Britain was not to lose the economic and social benefits of more air travel. The number of people using UK airports had tripled in the past 20 years. Though the rate of growth was slowing, the government forecast that demand would double within the next 20 years. However, the number of stakeholders involved in this contentious debate was huge.

Baroness Dean was asked to chair the campaign but had no experience of aviation apart from being a passenger: "They said that was exactly why they wanted me to do it. We had not had a government policy on aviation for over 50 years and they wanted a White Paper as the continentals were beating the socks off us."

They wanted someone who, when being interviewed, would not be accused of being partisan. "So I took it on for a year and it ended up being for two years," continues Baroness Dean. "At first I thought it was completely different from what I had done before and then I realised it wasn't."

She realised the importance of the aviation industry to the UK and of having an aviation policy: "We are good at aviation in the UK – we are an island and we need it. Therefore, much as people might be anti aviation, we do need a proper policy on the expansion of our goods and trade and also it is an industry that pays well at a time when a lot of people are working in call centres for low salaries. It is a good industry with good skills. So instinctively I was supportive, and when I got into it and realised how important it is for our economy, that was good. Also it is a good sector and when you look at what has happened to BT and some of our good blue-chip companies, Britain never seems content until it has beaten them over the head and beaten them out of existence. We seem to have to apologise for success."

On the negotiating side, Manchester had objected to Heathrow's application to expand. Baroness Dean explains: "Manchester thought it would take trade away from them and the industry did not get its act together. So what they did cleverly on this one was to get a White Paper on the Expansion of Aviation in the UK – something we could all sign up to."

They got all the airlines involved, the TUC, the CBI, everyone across the board. "The only people who were not in were the Greens and the rail unions and Transport 2000 which was basically rail based," continues Baroness Dean. "So I went to Bob Crowe and said, 'You can oppose this but actually it will probably mean more jobs for you because if Heathrow is expanded you will need a rail link from Heathrow and it will not take jobs away.' So we got them not to oppose and Transport 2000 were furious with us so we got them."

She recalls how people kept bringing in their own pet themes, to which she said, "No, our job is getting this focused, to get a White Paper on Aviation." The environmental lobby said it would be impossible to get expansion at Heathrow because of noise. "So we spoke quietly to the airlines and they said that the new generation of planes are going to be quieter, we need expansion because we are always circling London and doing more environmental damage. So we went quietly and gently and suggested that expansion would lead to a new generation of more environmentally friendly planes – the A380 for example – and less noise too."

It took two years but eventually they got what they wanted – a White Paper. It has been judged as the most successful campaign the aviation industry has ever had. This is a great example of mastery and its application. History now shows that from these roots the expansion of Heathrow did happen, with the opening of Terminal Five in 2008.

In Chapter 8, we identify areas of focus in our learning and development that can be applied to help with our DNA of Success. I have uncovered a key mental model around intelligence. This is a model that can be applied repeatedly in all forms of coaching, learning and personal development. It follows the pattern described above in that it provides a framework and can be articulated easily, yet it can and does have a depth and level of complexity that, without the framework, would be difficult to remember and recall.

So a key lesson from this success factor within mastery is to build a set of mental models around key areas of mastery.

Passion and drive around innovation

Two key elements of mastery emerge from my interviews with our contributors in terms of skills and beliefs around innovation. These show up most notably in one distinct area: innovation in their career and a desire to 'be the first'. Seeking to be the first is a key area of innovation and mastery. Our contributors display a passion in terms of seeking groundbreaking breakthroughs both for themselves and their organisations:

- Penny Hughes was the first woman vice president in Coca-Cola and the youngest to hold this position.
- Brenda Dean was the first woman president of a major trade union in the United Kingdom.
- Graham Taylor was the first person in football to make the journey from player to coach and then to the boardroom.
- Lord MacLaurin launched the first consumer loyalty scheme, which has now driven a path of acceptability of this type of consumer behaviour across global industries.
- Frederick Forsyth was the youngest-ever Royal Air Force pilot to get his wings on jets.
- Greg Dyke introduced the Freeview terrestrial digital transmission platform with six additional BBC channels in 2002 – this effectively changed the face of TV as we know it.

The second element that emerges from my interviews is the passion to move from research and planning to a rapid mindset of action, either with customers or people. Greg Dyke gave me a wonderful quote: "It's better to be known for what you tried to achieve than to be known for what you thought you could achieve but never did." The advice is to research to the point of clarity, look at options for contingency but then rapidly try it.

Our masters have the ability to put into practice and evolve what others spend a lifetime thinking about.

Investing in learning

All of our contributors have evolved their mastery continuously, based on a 'joy of learning'. Baroness Dean encapsulates this best when she talks about a key influence on her life: her school teacher George Booth, who we discussed in Chapter 1: "When I think about what I inherited from George it was about the joy of learning. I got the nickname 'Brenda Why' as I always wanted to know why and George was really the best of teachers and he was so important to us. Going forward, I always wanted to keep learning and keep testing myself and improving my learning ability. I lost touch with George but was lucky enough to make contact with him and meet him at The House before he sadly passed away. He was a great inspiration in terms of learning and its benefits."

When asked about the key skill of learning, Vince Cable says: "You have to be adaptable and certainly in a political world you have to be able to adapt. I'm now in my late sixties, but you always have to be prepared to learn and not to rest on your laurels; you have to be able to be constantly learning."

During my research I discovered a great fact while listening to Peter Thomson, who produces an audio publication called *The Achiever's Edge*: "If you read a book [on the same subject] a week for a year, you would become the 99 per cent expert in that subject." Daily investment in our learning can come from one hour a day practising in our area of mastery. We would think that we could never afford to spend that time on development, but if done a little at a time on a constant basis it's achievable. One hour a day turns into the equivalent of just over nine working weeks of training and development within a year.

Continuous learning and development is a key requirement for mastery.

The application of mastery

Concerning how our contributors have applied mastery to their careers in terms of the people and organisations they've led, four key themes emerge, which our contributors believed in and applied, and these are totally consistent:

1. Our contributors see leadership as part of the culture in an organisation, starting at grass-roots level not in the boardroom. The development of mastery works best through inspiration not authority, and through being a role model not through hierarchical pressure. Sir Peter Squire, talking about the military and leadership, best sums this up with "what people should do, not what they must do". Continuous development and the pursuit of mastery is demanding so it needs leadership to help nurture it.
2. Recognition and provision of a coaching culture in an organisation is key to mastery. This allows for the critical roles of teacher and coach and for feedback to happen and be encouraged. All our contributors had coaches or mentors and all see coaches and mentors as vital in their organisations.
3. Early identification of promising performers and the investment of significant time, money and energy in developing people are important. Each of our contributors had been 'fortunate' enough to have been spotted early in their careers, the most graphic examples of this being Penny Hughes – a vice president in a global enterprise, Coca-Cola, at 33 years of age – and Brenda Dean – a senior union official at 27 years of age. Our contributors recognise their personal drive to stand out at an early stage but also how important it is for help in this area.

4. Lastly, there is an absolute recognition that, while individual talent is key, developing teams in organisations is also vital. There needs to be an equal balance here for team development. The research around creating teams – not individuals – as a route to success in organisations would fill a book on its own. What is emergent here is that the recognition of this as a skill of mastery is not to be ignored in the sole pursuit of individual mastery.

Inevitably in the pursuit of mastery – even with the best creation of followship, with the best set of values in place and having had the wisdom passed on from mentors – there are times in life when things do not go according to plan and setbacks occur. The next two chapters take us through some of these times as experienced by our contributors as we cover the topics of persistence and transformational setbacks.

Chapter 5
Persistence

Persistence is a consistent attribute that emerges from the interviews with our contributors. This may not be a headline grabber or a groundbreaking revelation in terms of success, so why a chapter devoted to this topic? The answer lies in what it delivers.

My definition of 'persistence' is 'turning purpose and passion into personal success'. The basis of persistence is willpower. Willpower and passion, when properly combined, make an irresistible pair and, when aligned with a clear direction, are a major stepping stone to ensuring the attainment of successful goals and successful lives.

In this chapter we will look at four key areas:

1. Illustrate **persistence in action** by looking at an example of one man's remarkable perseverance in creating a global company.
2. Define **the seven key elements of persistence** that emerge from our contributors and highlight, within these seven elements, stories from our contributors to bring these to life.
3. Combine input from our contributors with research to produce a ten-point **persistence inventory** in terms of barriers to enabling persistence as a way of being. Included in this is a model I have used extensively in coaching, which I have found to be the number one development tool in enabling persistence.
4. Define and uncover a simple **persistence framework** to follow.

Persistence in action

My goal is to show that if persistence is a state of mind, then it can be learnt, developed and mastered. It will then become a habit that is part of the enablement of success. The elements we will cover give the 'how to do' based on my work to enable persistence to be a practical 'tool' and way of being.

By way of an introduction, in my research the most remarkable story around persistence came from a very unexpected source. It is the story of Howard Schultz and his perseverance in making Starbucks the global high street institution that it is today. Schultz has gone on to accumulate a net worth of over a billion dollars, but his journey started with a phenomenal example of persistence, which he acknowledges as a key attribute of his success. The story starts when Howard Schultz tried for a year to get a job at Starbucks, but failed.

At that time Starbucks comprised just three shops in Seattle, selling coffee beans, coffee makers and coffee paraphernalia, but not coffee by the cup. Schultz was a coffee maker salesman for a Swedish company when he heard of this little-known store in Seattle that was selling more coffee makers than Macy's. He was so swept up in the ambience, the romance and the passion that they had for their coffee business that he wanted to work there, but it took him a year to get the job.

He spent a year roasting and serving up beans, and he spent another year trying to convince them to sell coffee by the cup, but they refused. Finally, they allowed one espresso machine and started selling; it was so successful that they could sell as much coffee as they could supply to their customers. However, the founders still didn't want to turn the shop into a coffee bar. In 1985 Schultz, still devoted to his dream, left to start his own coffee shop called 'Il Giornale' and he had to talk to 242 investors before he had enough money to launch it. Two years later, the original Starbucks management decided to focus on 'Peet's Coffee & Tea' and sold its Starbucks retail units to Schultz and Il Giornale for $3.8 million.

Today, Starbucks has an astounding 16,858 locations worldwide, including 11,131 in the United States. Howard Schultz's story and the following quote capture the essence of perseverance: "How many people have you met in your life who have said 'I had that idea', 'I knew about that' or 'I was so close but I gave up'? Sometimes I think the difference between success and failure, winning and losing is a fine line between those people who will continue to move forward and those that quit early."

The seven key elements of persistence

Persistence can be linked to definite mindsets, actions and behaviour. I have linked these to my research and interpreted, prioritised and produced a

DNA principles framework, as follows:

1. **Definiteness of purpose.** Knowing what we want is the first and perhaps the most important step towards the development of persistence. A strong motivational force, underpinning and driving that purpose, is a key requirement in order to surmount any difficulties or setbacks ... **purpose ignites the spirit**. A graphic example of knowing one's purpose and having a definite view on the direction for that purpose is shown in the story of Baroness Dean. Her persistence over a 20-year period was about overcoming prejudice against a woman in a man's world, the world of trade unions. She never took her eye off the goal of becoming the leader of a major trade union, SOGAT, and perseverance and the application and continual, relentless focus on her goal comes through her life story.

2. **Passion.** With this in place, it is comparatively easy to acquire and maintain persistence in pursuing the object of our intense passion ... **passion gives inexhaustible energy**.

3. **Belief.** A belief in our ability to carry out a plan drives, maintains and encourages us to follow the plan through with persistence ... **belief sustains the journey**. My best example from my interviews of the link between belief and perseverance involves Greg Dyke. Dyke's persistence in following his chosen path of broadcasting, for many years with several companies, eventually led him to a major role within the BBC. It was here that he experienced a very public setback, but his perseverance 'kicked back in' and allowed him to reshape his outcome to a new direction in terms of career. This is a great example of persistence but ensuring that the persistence is aligned to and constantly checked against the desired goal and outcome.

4. **Definiteness of plans.** Organised plans, even though they may need to be revised, updated and changed, enable persistence. Without a plan, the ability to persist becomes weaker ... **preparation builds the foundation**.

5. **Accurate knowledge.** Knowing that the plans are sound and based upon experience encourages persistence. The enemy of persistence is guessing instead of knowing ... **knowledge removes uncertainty in the mind**.

6. **Co-operation.** The ability to work with others allows persistence to develop and multiply, and gives an extra motivational input, particularly in times of difficulty. Working in co-operation with others unlocks purpose, passion and power in others ... **teams strengthen the belief.** A great example of this from my interviews concerns the journey of Vince Cable from corporate life to becoming a Member of Parliament, as it illustrates not only how we need others on this journey but also the value of sheer perseverance. Cable put himself up for election five times, over a 15-year period, before finally being elected as an MP: "In my case persistence is a value and also a way of being. Stamina and a lot of help from my late wife, who would put up with a huge amount of disruption to our lives, helped me make it through. There was a danger that I might have dropped out altogether had it not been for her support. The support and motivation I received from others was a major factor in my determination and persistence to make it into the world of politics as a Member of Parliament."

7. **Willpower.** The habit of concentrating our thoughts on attaining a definitive purpose drives, energises and sustains persistence ... **strength of willpower is the foundation for perseverance.** Graham Taylor, whose story about overcoming a very public setback in his time as international football manager is captured in Chapter 6, sums up the importance of perseverance as a key attribute for success in the following quote, which encapsulates willpower and the spirit of perseverance as a mindset: "I'm not a deeply religious man, but I think I have beliefs and values that have helped me overcome setbacks. However, one thing I know to be true: the Good Samaritan picks you up off the ground and I have to say that can happen. But he does not do it unless he sees that you start to get up yourself. If you have been knocked down and you are flat out and show no effort to get back up I think the Good Samaritan will walk straight past you. When I look back on my life, the England setback was a defining moment: perseverance and sheer willpower to succeed and come through that was a great characteristic I could draw from."

The most comprehensive inventory of persistence is found in the book *Think and Grow Rich* by Napoleon Hill. He was inspired by Andrew Carnegie, whom he used as a role model. Hill spent a lifetime of research interviewing 500 wealthy men and women, who revealed the source of their thoughts, ideas and plans. The book is timeless and as practical today as when it was first published in 1937.

Hill's book is predominantly about 'what to do' and 'how to do it', which aligns with the philosophy behind *The DNA of Success*. He devotes a chapter to persistence and his persistence inventory, which we now cover. This again gives an exact match in a number of areas to the views and experiences of our contributors.

The persistence inventory can be used as an education platform so that the seven habits mentioned in the previous section become part of a persistence mentality and way of being. The framework is in ten parts:

1. Fear of criticism
Failure to create plans and to put them into action because of what other people will think, do or say belongs at the top of the list to address, as it is usually buried deep in the subconscious and linked to a limiting belief. I have found through coaching that once this limiting belief is brought into awareness, this barrier can successfully be removed.

2. Procrastination
This is the habit of replacing high-priority items with tasks of low priority and therefore putting off important tasks to a later time or, worse, never undertaking them. The habit is usually reinforced with a considerable amount of alibis and excuses, and results in stress, a sense of guilt and crises repeatedly occurring, severe loss of personal productivity, and often peer or social disapproval as responsibilities or commitments are not met.

It's often a self-fulfilling cycle, as once the pattern is established the temptation to further procrastinate is heightened by the symptoms themselves. None of our contributors operate in any way, shape or form in the 'area' of procrastination; several did balance decision making by taking multiple inputs, but this was done over a shortened period of time.

In Hill's view, "Those suffering with procrastination had often a low sense of self-worth and a self-defeating mentality. Procrastination is the enemy of success."

3. Lack of organised plans

It is essential to have organised plans that can be monitored and analysed on an ongoing basis as an aid to the achievement of your goals. The lack of these is a barrier to success.

4. The habit of not recognising or not moving on ideas or opportunities when they present themselves

Chapter 7 covers a key attribute for the DNA of Success, which I have termed 'synchronicity'. This directly aligns to 'seizing the moment' and is one of the top repeatable success attributes illustrated in the experiences and success of all our contributors.

5. Poor motivational direction resulting in lack of passion

My personal coach, Jamie Smart, who runs an excellent organisation for personal coaching called Salad (www.saladltd.co.uk) has a very powerful, but simple, framework that captures this. He refers to this as "start where you want to end". Smart's model is called the 'focus creation cycle' and we can use this at a strategic, tactical and personal level to underpin how we create belief that is aligned to emotions, actions and a 'laser-like' focus. The belief is underpinned by the emotional driver which is the key to producing action. Smart says: "People only do what they are motivated by and the action is a direct result and correlation to the strength of the motivation."

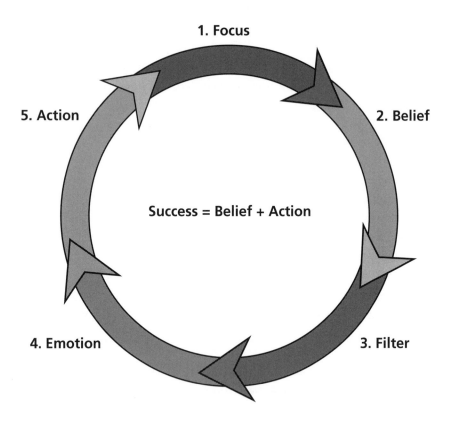

1. Focus

5. Action

2. Belief

Success = Belief + Action

4. Emotion

3. Filter

The focus creation cycle can be broken down into five elements: focus, belief, the filter, emotion and action.

Focus

In organisations (and indeed in life), whatever we focus on we tend to get. The mindset of our people, and therefore our organisation, has to be set up to focus on success and what we want to achieve. It is very destructive to focus on a negative goal, as by its very nature it focuses attention on the very thing we don't want!

For example, being rated the number one company in our industry for customer service is a clear, positive goal. A less specific and less positive goal, for example "not being in the bottom five rated companies in our industry", inadvertently focuses attention on what we don't want to achieve. In other words – we can't do a don't!

It is essential to focus and communicate the messages in our organisation on what we do want. Focus is an organisational amplifier. Make sure that it is focused on what we do want to achieve.

Belief

I am sure that you will be familiar with the glass metaphor regarding people's attitudes – the concept of whether they regard the glass as being 'half empty' (a negative/pessimistic attitude) or 'half full' (a positive/optimistic attitude). For the purposes of the model, we can describe people's thinking strategies as tending to lead them to adopting one or other of these positions. Whether we think the glass is half full or half empty will affect how we experience the world.

The filter

Writer and teacher Leonard Orr, building on the work of Robert Anton Wilson in his book *Prometheus Rising*, has modelled the human mind as having two aspects – a 'thinker' and a 'prover'. He describes this concept as "whatever the thinker thinks, the prover proves". That is, our beliefs ('the thinker') act as a filter through which all incoming data is processed. We unconsciously select evidence that supports our beliefs ('the prover') and filter out any data that is contrary to them.

The part of our mind modelled as the prover will only provide evidence that proves we are right. If we believe we can't do something, then our prover will sort and filter all incoming data to prove that belief to be true.

If we believe that we can make a great difference in our personal development, then our prover will find evidence to support that empowering belief. However, if we believe that we cannot make any difference, then our prover will go to work to prove us correct. Or, as Henry Ford once said: "If you think you can or think you can't, you're right."

To explore the 'thinker/prover' model further, I recommend Robert Anton Wilson's book *Prometheus Rising*.

Emotion

Emotion is the key that turns focus into action. Emotions are amplifiers; they are a driving force that increases what we focus on. Unfortunately, negative emotions, such as worry, amplify the focus as well.

We can turn emotions to our advantage by eliciting the positive emotions that will occur when we reach, for example, some of our organisational goals and then recognise our people accordingly. Then we can generate positive emotions such as pride, self-fulfilment, sense of achievement and self-worth. These positive emotions will help to create a positive sense of hunger and desire for future success and turn the focus into actions that everyone follows and completes.

When I was at Dell during its early days, the vision and focus of the company was to be "the number one PC supplier in each geographical region" by comparison with where IBM and Compaq were at the time. This looked challenging and a long haul. However, the goal was utilised to create positive emotional benefits. The people involved wanted to feel the pride and fulfilment of winning such an uphill battle.

Whether to fulfil personal emotions of being part of the best team, to feel an individual sense of achievement or to earn bonuses, people mobilised behind the 'emotional pull' and vision of being number one. The goal was to take the number one position in three years. It was achieved in two years. Emotions link positive focus to winning actions.

Action

However strong the focus, belief and emotion, without action nothing much will change! Our actions have to support what we are focusing on. The actions then give us the evidence that what we have been focusing on is turning into reality and this then turbo-boosts the process as the cycle starts again.

To remember this focus creation cycle, think of it as a simple equation: **Success = Belief + Action**. The focus creation cycle is a valuable model to use to create motivational direction as a key success attribute in persistence.

6. Searching for shortcuts
This is about trying to get by with continual risk-taking without analysing the plans or consequences.

7. Indifference
This is characterised by readiness to compromise on all occasions rather than meeting the 'opposition' and fighting for the cause or goal.

8. Blaming others
This is when we blame others continually for mistakes and look at circumstances as the causes of failure rather than looking at the plan, the goal, the vision and the implementation.

9. No desire to acquire specialist knowledge and mastery
We have covered mastery, and its absolute importance to the DNA of Success, in Chapter 4. Without the willpower and persistence in wanting to acquire specialist skills, behaviours and knowledge, persistence will not be a habit.

10. Willingness to quit at the first sign of defeat or setback
Persistence is enabled and necessary to overcome this debilitating behaviour in terms of the DNA of Success.

Persistence framework

The next step in this DNA of Success attribute is to define a process and framework that will lead to the habit of persistence. When I questioned our contributors, as always with people who are enabled and experts at a particular behaviour, I discovered that they do not recognise that they are using a framework. However, with further questioning, I discovered a definite sequence:

1. A definite purpose and the motivation to deliver it need to be in place. The use of the focus creation model can be an added extra here (to help achieve this).
2. The plan expressed in key action areas can then be developed.
3. Our contributors do not consider or work within a negative framework and they keep their minds closed to negativity, including from close sources. Instead, they focus on success and how to achieve it. This does not mean that they ignore possible downsides, but they put on a success consciousness and define plans based on success rather than failure. In Chapter 3 we discussed how 'managing fear consciousness' and 'creating success consciousness' are two key elements of creating a leadership mindset for ourselves and also to enable others to be inspired and follow.
4. Nobody can succeed alone; the plan needs to include alliances and co-operation with others. All of our contributors are always inclusive and involve others in their plans and visions.

Once these four steps are in place, they can be repeated in multiple situations and opportunities over time.

To summarise this chapter, we have looked at breaking down the seven key attributes of perseverance into how we define it, how people have used perseverance in the pursuit of success, and tools around diagnosis/inventory and a framework for putting it into practice. The stories from our contributors all show that perseverance is a key on the road to success and successful lives.

The next chapter shows persistence in action in terms of being one of the necessities in overcoming and using setbacks as a transformational and tipping point for success.

During my interviews, one of the key themes that emerged as a consistent success factor was our contributors' ability to overcome shattering, high-impact setbacks. Based on these interviews, I have put together a DNA of Success blueprint that will provide an inspirational and highly practical set of insights into how to tackle setbacks and be a learning tool for those with whom we work.

I have identified six elements, each providing standalone learning and together forming an integrated blueprint for overcoming setbacks as a necessary part of our journey through adversity to success. These six elements are as follows:

- Defining a purpose
- A question of trust
- Self-belief
- Rapid exit
- Success consciousness
- Stickability.

These elements are covered one by one within this chapter, illustrated with graphic examples provided by our contributors' stories around setbacks in order to breathe life into this fascinating subject.

Throughout my research and when reading the autobiographies of great achievers in business, sport and literature, there is an undeniable trait that sets the truly successful person apart. It is the ability to push through times of adversity and to use those times as a learning zone and simply see them as part of the success journey. They are not a reason to quit.

Books full of quotes and stories about overcoming adversity are not rare, but my approach is to allow the DNA of Success to emerge so that we can use it as something valuable for each and every one of us in whatever way we choose. However, there is one independent quote, from Nelson Mandela, always worthy of inclusion, to start our thoughts moving in an inspirational way through this chapter: "The greatest glory in living lies not in never falling, but in rising every time we fall."

Mandela, the leading anti-apartheid activist in white-dominated South Africa, was sentenced to life imprisonment in 1962 and served 27 years, 18 as a classification D prisoner – the toughest scale – in the notorious Robben Island Prison. Released in 1990, he returned to lead his party in negotiations that led to multi-racial democracy in 1994. He was 72 when he became South Africa's first black, democratically elected South African president. He has been, and still is, the best example of overcoming setbacks, keeping faith, passion and focus alive, and transforming setbacks into achievements that have touched the lives of millions.

Defining a purpose

Knowing what we want is perhaps the most important step towards the development of the skill, behaviour and mindset needed to overcome setbacks and how to use those setbacks as tipping points in life to propel us to success. This strong motivational force allows us to surmount our difficulties. Our contributors can articulate their 'end in mind' throughout their careers in terms of their roles and achievements. This resolve and focus is a driving factor enabling them to overcome short-term setbacks. It comes across clearly that this focus is key to the successful outcomes enjoyed in their careers once the problem was overcome.

According to Greg Dyke, what makes us lucky and able to survive is a belief in ourselves and the belief that our life is our own: "Don't do what others want you to do; do what **you** want to do. The world is full of timid people afraid to make decisions or stand up for what's right. I am lucky in that I do not suffer from that – and that's what has helped me move on in my life."

Dyke resigned from the BBC as Director General on 29 January 2004 after the publication of the Hutton Report. Hutton described Dyke's approach to checking news stories as "defective"; when Alastair Campbell complained about the story (the Iraq War), Dyke had immediately defended it without investigating whether there was any merit to the complaint.

In an email sent to all BBC staff just prior to his resignation, Dyke wrote: "I accept that the BBC made errors of judgement and I've sadly come to the conclusion that it will be hard to draw a line under this whole affair while I am still here. We need closure. We need closure to protect the future of the BBC, not for you or me but for the benefit of everyone out there. It might sound pompous but I believe the BBC really matters."

It was subsequently established that Dyke had offered his resignation to the BBC's board of governors while hoping that they would reject it. However, he was only able to secure the support of about one-third of the governors. Some BBC staff felt that their organisation had been given too much blame for the David Kelly affair in the Hutton Report. Groups of staff stood outside Broadcasting House and other BBC centres across the country, protesting at the unfairness. Speaking on *GMTV* on 30 January, Dyke himself questioned the conclusions of the report, saying: "We were shocked it was so black and white [...] we knew mistakes had been made but we didn't believe they were only by us." He also claimed that Lord Hutton was "quite clearly wrong" on certain aspects of law relating to the case.

This episode was obviously a major setback and it was publicly played out in front of the world media. What insights can Dyke offer in terms of our perspective on success and overcoming? He says: "Looking back I have had a few setbacks. Getting sacked at 18 was not really great even though I was secretly delighted (as I hated the job). When I was CEO of LWT and we lost London Weekend in a hostile takeover bid, they asked me to stay on as MD. I said to the CEO, 'No way, you are the enemy as far as I am concerned,' so the next day there I was, at home, taking the kids to school and meeting them after school."

It meant that by the time he went to the "savage community" of the BBC, he had learnt to survive: "I knew I could survive setbacks. Those are the experiences that are the test. How do you come through at the end? You have to experience it in order to know. Like the footballer who breaks his leg for the first time, you have got to know that you will get through it. Some people find it harder than others. I think I have been fairly lucky in life. I think you need to be lucky in life. I have four nice kids – I have had fun jobs in management. I went straight from making programmes to running a company, really. You have got to have luck in life."

Dyke's burning self-belief and confidence is very evident and, as he stated above, this is a key belief that has enabled him to go through a number of transformational setbacks.

A question of trust

A key element that emerges from our contributors' stories is that of unwavering trust in their own belief system and knowing when to listen to their inner voice. There are three levels of trust: our gut instinct, our inner dialogue and our 'inner' best friend in times of crisis and where decisions of magnitude need to be made.

Sir Peter Squire best sums this up when he was faced with a career-changing decision around whether to trust his gut instinct that the Red Arrows leadership was not for him and not in the best interest of the team. Initially he ignored his gut feeling that it was the wrong position for him at the time. Fortunately, he revisited that decision and moved on. This proved to be a key move in his career and a good outcome for the Red Arrows. It was based on a true gut instinct.

"I was coming towards the end of my second tour and I was an instructor teaching people to fly a plane called the Hunter operating out of Anglesey. I had done three years of solo display aerobatics and at weekends doing air shows, etc. I had a phone call on a Friday evening from someone in HQ from Training Command and they asked if I would like to take over leadership of the Red Arrows," explains Sir Peter.

He was not sure whether he wanted to do it as he really wanted to get back to the operational front line. So he said to the person who had asked him: "Can I think about it over the weekend and let you know on Monday?" He was obviously not expecting that answer!

Sir Peter discussed it with his wife, Carolyn, at the weekend and they decided that he would say 'No'. Not long after the call, he was summoned by the Air Secretary's Department – a sort of promotions and postings board – who said: "We are not sure you fully understood what you said 'no' to." They tried to persuade him to think again and he went to see the person who had originally phoned and eventually he was persuaded to take the job.

"This was in the September of 1973 and I went to join the Red Arrows team," says Sir Peter. "I had never been on the team before and they had never had a leader who had not come up through their ranks so they were not particularly happy about my selection. It had been imposed on them rather than their having had a say. So I arrived and clearly there was an atmosphere. Actually, I probably was not the right person for the job. The difficulty was compounded by the imposition of the three-day working week – the year Heath challenged the miners. So when the three-day week took place, the Air Force said, 'Sorry, public opinion says you have got to stop training as we cannot be seen to be wasting fuel'."

So from November until about March they did not do any flying and by the time they started again, although they worked hard, it was clear that the team would not be ready to start a display season at the beginning of May. Sir Peter continues the story: "The Air Force did not mind – they said as long as we were ready for Farnborough in September that was OK. I said: 'Frankly, it is not fine by me and really I should leave and you should bring back the chap who led it last year who will probably get them going quicker than I will,' and that is what they did."

So he resigned from the team. "That could have been quite a blow – but fortunately the Air Force seemed to recognise the sense of it and I was posted quickly on to Harriers, which was exactly the plane I wanted to fly. I went off and did a flight commander's job in Germany and then was selected to command No. 1 Squadron operating out of the UK in 1981. This meant that I led that squadron to war in the Falklands. So if I had made a go of the Red Arrows I would never have been in the position to command No. 1 Squadron in 1981. And I will always maintain that, while I regret that the arrows tour did not work out, not to have commanded No.1 Squadron in 1982 would have been a greater disappointment. My experience during the Falklands Conflict – flying combat missions from an aircraft carrier – made me somewhat unusual in the RAF of the Cold War era. It gave me a profile that set me apart from others."

Brenda Dean, equally, when faced with an easy, financially attractive job which was also a route away from a setback, trusted her inner voice and waited for the right move. "My major setback occurred when circumstances dictated that the two major print unions were to be merged – NGA and SOGAT. This meant we had two leaders running for one position and I lost out. Tony Dubbins became general secretary and I became the number two," she says.

Although she accepted the outcome, she was not happy being number two: "I had thoughts such as, 'Who is going to employ me? I am known as a firebrand; am I employable? What transferable skills do I have?' These were questions I was always asking myself. It was a real dip for me and you get that feeling of rejection."

However, the job offers did come in and one in particular was outstanding in terms of pay and rewards. She continues: "However, I was not excited about it in other ways and I could not work out why I did not go for it. But my inner voice told me to let it go and I knew I should wait for the right opportunity. The great lesson for me is being sure what you want and then going for it. Don't compromise and take the first opportunity. Deal with your failures and use them to learn and move on to what you want to achieve. It's the failures that make us who we are."

This is exactly what Greg Dyke said in his interview – never settle for second best and do what you want to do.

Frederick Forsyth also came through two major setbacks – one professional, one personal. The professional setback involved his time as a BBC reporter in war-torn Biafra in the late 1960s. This was caused by the attempted secession of the south-eastern provinces of Nigeria as the self proclaimed Republic of Biafra. I'll allow Forsyth to take up the story from here: "Before I departed for the rebel enclave I had been given an extremely copious briefing as to what I would find and what was going on; plus what was going to happen. I did not know until later this briefing at Broadcasting House came from the world service (West Africa division). They got it from the commonwealth relations office who got it from our High Commissioner in Lagos, Sir David Hunt. On arrival I only needed a pair of eyes and ears to see it was utter and complete nonsense. Unwisely I said so and it was broadcast and heard loud and clear in Lagos. The High Commissioner went completely spare and flew back from London to complain bitterly." Forsyth believed that he was right and resigned, and went back as a freelance journalist for a further two years. The conflict, which was referred to as 'a storm in a teacup' by the establishment lasted two and a half years and killed up to a million Biafran children.

On a personal front, Frederick Forsyth had a major setback in 1990: "I lost every penny I had through being embezzled by a personal friend. I ended up bankrupt at 50. One of Forsyth's key values is tenacity and this is an example of where he had to turn it from a value into action.

Self-belief

One of the qualities to emerge from our contributors' stories is an unwavering sense of self-belief. Because they are high-profile people, the setbacks were usually accompanied by huge media attention and focus.

Graham Taylor experienced this through the press attack in his time as England manager, as did Brenda Dean through the many personal intrusions into her life when she was battling with the newspaper owners, and more recently Greg Dyke was the focus of the media at the time of the Hutton Inquiry and his exit from the BBC. Penny Hughes had difficult decisions to make both in her time at Coca-Cola and at Vodafone, as does Vince Cable who lives in the eye of the media as a current serving minister and politician.

What I have found in interviewing our contributors is that this media focus actually intensifies self-belief. Most people would not wish to be put through this, but a high level of self-belief is definitely a key requirement in moving through these setbacks and onwards towards success. The second element within this category is the link between self-belief and doing the right thing. Our contributors all ignored short-term gain and did not allow themselves to be forced to compromise over what they believed in. When Sir Peter resigned as leader of the Red Arrows, it was potentially a career-limiting move. But he knew that it was the right thing to do and had true self-belief allied to knowing that it was best for the team and his country. All of our contributors have displayed amazing examples of courage – not courage in terms of individual acts of bravery, but more courage of conviction – to overcome what could have been either career-ending or life-changing setbacks.

Brenda Dean epitomises this by showing great courage in order to establish herself as the first woman leader of a trade union. She also had to establish herself as a woman in a man's world at a time when that was a groundbreaking achievement.

Rapid exit

Every failure brings with it the seeds of equivalent success. Our contributors have a firm belief that any setback is just a 'temporary defeat'. They are all able to make a rapid exit from any situation if it's the wrong one – irrespective of short-term consequences. The avoidance of procrastination over a decision is a key attribute of success in overcoming setbacks. Penny Hughes and her story around 'Tab' clearly illustrates that, even on a global level, rapid exit is better than a long drawn-out failure. She firmly believes in "moving forward".

Hughes was the first woman and youngest-ever vice president of Coca-Cola at the age of 33. Her career has been a series of firsts, as we covered in Chapter 1. However, her time at the global brand Coca-Cola was formative in establishing her career direction. Here we cover her insights on overcoming setbacks and, in particular, a product launch that was disastrous: "I launched a brand at Coca-Cola called 'Tab Clear', which was a clear cola. It failed. But you learn from that experience. They did not kill me for it! So there are things you do in life that do not go well. I was the leader and I was accountable for a launch that did not work."

So, what did she learn from this experience? "I think if you have made a mistake you have to work it out quite quickly; you must define what you are going to do and face up to the reality, whatever it is. So we launched with great aplomb, and made a lot of noise – but the product just did not deliver – there was just not the enthusiasm for it. So we withdrew. You apply a speedy decision and reverse out."

According to Hughes, it is important to learn from mistakes and then move on: "One of the things that makes me know I am different in dealing with setbacks is that I stopped learning history a long time ago – I did not even get to 'O' level history – I had no interest in it. A lot of business people I know have an enormous interest in history and often might share books about this, that and the other. They often read military plans as a sort of alternative way of mapping out businesses. I can't come close to that! But I do learn from mistakes and so in a way I do learn from history – but 90% of the time I am thinking about the future and making history! I am not encumbered by the past. I would ask people: 'If you think you are always looking at things in hindsight, viewing things from a historical viewpoint, does it leave you backward looking?'"

So, would she launch another brand next week? "Absolutely. Things are always different every time you do them. You have to keep moving forward. Of course I learn from mistakes and what has gone before, but in order that I can equip myself to make better decisions going forward, I hope I spend most of my time thinking about going forward rather than looking back. So that is an optimistic view too. I am a glass half full person. I learn, adapt, then move on. In a way, because I have got a pretty clear vision of whatever business I am in, these are just little setbacks. These are just things you come across along the journey. The journey is still clear to me."

Hughes moved on from Coca-Cola to become the most experienced non-executive director operating on global boards for the past 16 years and her insight here into accountability, rapid exit and positive forward focus when dealing with setbacks is valuable in our search for the DNA of Success.

My summary of this attitude is that the tipping point of success is often through a crisis or a failure. Temporary defeat should only mean one thing:

there is something wrong with the plan but not necessarily the idea or the direction.

Success consciousness

Success comes to those who are success conscious, not failure conscious. For example, Thomas Edison experienced 10,000 failures before he had success in inventing the light bulb; his view was: "I had 9,999 attempts to get it right first." This is a fundamental mindset needed to come through setbacks, and one that is displayed by all our contributors: they all think of success not failure. We can think of this as success consciousness.

When I asked Greg Dyke about his view on the people he's worked with and the lessons he's learnt over his career, his answer was simply: "Employ positive people and do not compromise on this as a key requirement." Graham Taylor has achieved so much in the world of international football and subsequently as a respected media commentator. He tells a truly moving story around his transformational setback. Taylor has a value he lives by and a great quote: "Quitters never win – winners never quit." That is not just an idle quote but it encompasses Taylor's values and the way he came through what was a personal crisis for him and his family.

Taylor describes his major transformational setback as being at the end of his time as England manager. But he was prepared for this by a life lesson he learnt when he failed to be selected for the England Schoolboys Team when he was in his teens: "I remember hearing that I was not selected from one of my teachers – Mr Hill – and his words still ring true to this day. 'Taylor,' he said, 'Face it – it is a disappointment, and you will get more of those in life. Deal with it, even if you feel you have not been fairly represented.' I know it did me good."

To set the story in context, Taylor was appointed the England manager in 1990 and left the role in November 1993. He was in charge of the national team for 38 games, with 18 wins, 13 draws and 7 losses. However, it was ultimately the failure of the national team to qualify for the World Cup finals in the USA, a poor performance in the European championships, and a loss to the USA – relative minnows in football terms – that caused him to lose his job as England manager in 1993.

During this time, Taylor was involved in what is historically recognised as the most savage and vicious attack on a football manager ever taken on by the media. The headlines were personal, and the pursuit of Taylor and his family was unrelenting to the point that, during a tournament in the USA, his wife Rita rang to say that she could not even enter the family home as the driveway was so full of press and media.

So, in terms of a transformational event, here is what Taylor has to say: "For me to have been selected as England manager was a massive privilege and the confirmation of my standing within the game. It was the highest accolade and something I'm immensely proud of. However, the failure to qualify for the World Cup in 1994 and the poor performances at a major championship led me for the first time in my career to realise I had failed. This was a huge brick wall for me – and it was at the peak of my career and I realised I had to resurrect myself. I was public enemy number one because of the non-qualification for the World Cup in the USA. I remember thinking, 'What are you going to do, Graham?'"

The answer was to work very hard. Taylor continues: "It would have been very easy to walk away and leave the country but I never felt I should do this. There was no reason why England's failure in the World Cup should make me leave the country I loved, even though the abuse I was receiving was manifold."

His earlier life had prepared him for setbacks: "It is how you deal with them and how you come back."

Taylor's recovery was helped by the support he received from the public: "The media treatment I had received was a massive part of the situation. Looking back now I can clearly see that this was at the time of the Murdoch versus Maxwell media struggles for power and part of what happened to me was that I was a victim of this. However, what I learnt was that once the media go beyond what is acceptable to the public, the public fight back and part of my recovery and overcoming this setback was through the public support I received."

Taylor had not lost his self-belief: "Nor had I lost what I had achieved and what I still wanted to achieve. So I set about resurrecting my career." He achieved great success once again by taking Watford to the Premiership against the expectation of many experts.

Support from his family and his absolute belief in his own abilities also helped him through the situation: "No football manager will be a success without a good team and it is the same in most aspects of life. It is also important to take on responsibility for mistakes and to accept criticism. In sport, most people think they can do your job better than you, and at the same time your personal life becomes public. You may not like it – but that is how it is."

Taylor concludes: "[Managing England] is often described as the most impossible job, and subsequent managers will probably chuckle when they read this and I am sure they may well agree. However, for me it was the highest accolade and I learnt a tremendous amount about myself. It set me up to go on to achieve the success with Watford and in my later career as broadcaster and journalist."

Stickability ... three feet from gold

In my research into key attributes of success, I came across a fascinating story in the book *Think and Grow Rich* by Napoleon Hill, who is acknowledged as a thought leader in the world of self-development. His book, based on Andrew Carnegie's' magic formula for success, states that: "one of the most common causes of failure is the habit of quitting when one is taken over by temporary defeat. Every person is guilty of this mistake at one time or another."

He goes on to tell the story of a group of gold diggers and their quest for the elusive pot of gold in the days of the gold rush in Colorado. After weeks of labour they were rewarded by the discovery of shining ore, but they needed machinery to bring the gold to the surface in quantity. I will now let Hill tell the story. "The team went back to their relatives and neighbours to collect the necessary finance for the machinery and had it shipped to the mine. The first car of ore was mined and shipped to a smelter. The returns proved they had one of the richest mines in Colorado. A few more cars of that ore would clear the debts and give them a big killing in profits. Down went the drills! Up went their hopes! Then something happened; the vein of gold then disappeared! They had come to the end of the rainbow and the pot of gold was no longer there. They drilled on desperately to try and pick up the vein of gold again, but to no avail. Finally they quit. They sold the machinery to a junk man for a few hundred dollars and took the train for the long journey back home. The junk man called in a mining engineer [who] advised that the project had failed because the owners were not familiar with fault lines. His calculations showed that the vein would be found just three feet from where they had stopped drilling. That is exactly where it was found! The junk man took millions of dollars in ore from the mine, because he knew enough to seek expert counselling before giving up."

We can all ask ourselves how many times we have stopped 'just three feet from gold'. What I found in my interviews was that our contributors did not give up when faced by setbacks; this stickability is an essential attribute for overcoming setbacks. Stickability is probably best illustrated by the stories of Vince Cable and Baroness Dean.

Cable had to overcome a mass of setbacks and challenges in order to become a Member of Parliament. His success came after no fewer than five election campaigns. He puts this down to "persistence and support". He recalls what was behind his thinking and how he kept on track in terms of his ultimate goal of becoming an elected MP: "How did I keep going and motivated towards my aim? In my case it was persistence. Also stamina and a lot of help from my late wife, who put up with a lot of stuff – particularly during the York campaigns with all the travel and being away from home a great deal. She was so very tolerant and I think that without a supportive wife I would not have been able to do it. She had cancer and I spent a lot of time caring for her and it was quite difficult. There was a danger that I might have dropped out altogether had it not been for my wife and my two election campaigners."

What kept him going? "I would say that trying for a seat five times is more than persistence. You have got to be so dedicated." Did he know that he would eventually succeed? "No – I always hoped but I did not know I would succeed. I think it was feeling that I had spent so much time and effort and that others had also done so – not least my late wife – that I was going to disappoint too many people if I gave up."

Baroness Dean's fight against prejudice and discrimination is a classic tale of stickability. She had not been able to attend the local grammar school, having just failed to make the grade. However, she had a good education at her local school and great teachers who were an important influence on her. So she entered trade union life, which is where the story starts in terms of her looking at how setbacks, and the way she dealt with them, have shaped her success: "Well, getting over the grammar school disappointment was the first one. I really wanted to do it; I knew it might be a chance. I was not sure what for, I did not even know at that stage that I wanted to do better in life. That was the first one …. Interestingly, people did not see me as a threat. They never thought I could do any of these big roles so when there was an officer's job available in Manchester, I never even thought I could stand for it."

But Joe Sheriden (who had been her union boss) had warmed to her and started to act as a sponsor: "He said, 'Go for it,' so I did. It was an assistant's job. So I went for it and I got elected. I was 28 when I got the job as assistant secretary in Manchester, by which time Joe was seriously ill with a heart condition. He did not want anyone to know, so I was covering for him all the time, which meant I was taking on even more responsibility than I would have had he been well. Then he collapsed and died and so the big question was, who would get the big job in Manchester?"

That's when Baroness Dean came up against some real chauvinism: "I was obviously emotionally upset. When he [Joe] collapsed and died, I went to hospital with him – I knew he had died because of the way the ambulance men looked at one another. That was on a Friday and so when I got home (I had my own house by then) Dad was waiting for me with a couple of sleeping pills. I was very upset indeed. He said he wanted me to take these and go to bed and that he would stay all weekend. But of course the phone started ringing and so I knew I could not leave things in the air and I called a branch committee meeting for the Monday. All day on the Sunday I started to get calls, 'Don't worry, we will look after you' and 'Don't worry about this or that, there will be people wanting this position and people in that position' ... so the men were all fighting for position because it never occurred to them that I might stand for the job."

Baroness Dean describes this as her first real awakening: "If you had asked me on that Sunday if I was going to stand for the job I probably would have said 'No', but in a way it started to dawn on me that they did not see me in the role. So then, and I suppose I was pretty ruthless really, I forced myself to think about it and came to the conclusion that if any of them got the job and I stayed where I was, I would still be doing their job for them, while they took the praise. So I assessed what I could do and I thought, 'I can do it as well as they can.'"

At the meeting on Monday morning, Baroness Dean was appointed stand-in secretary. She continues her story: "So I said that this week we should have a week of mourning – Joe was an institution – and the funeral would be at the end of the week. Joe's family would organise that, but we would also be involved as it would be a big affair in the cathedral with a cortège. It would be a big funeral – it would stop Manchester. So we used our office admin backup to arrange things."

They agreed to meet again the following week and Baroness Dean announced her candidature for the job: "The chairman said something, I can't remember exactly what, along the lines of, 'Is Brenda going to stand as the branch secretary?' and I said, 'Of course I am – I AM the acting secretary and I know that there are people in this room who want to stand for the job and that is fine, but in the meantime I will get on with it. And if anyone comes out of the woodwork I have a bloody big hammer and I will hammer them back in – I AM the secretary; let's be clear about that.'"

There was some opposition but Baroness Dean won the job hands down, winning more votes than all the other candidates put together. Then several things happened. The first was a clear demonstration of chauvinism: "The *Manchester Evening News* turned up and wanted to take a picture. I was of course flattered; it was good for the union. So the photographer said to me, 'Would you mind sitting on the edge of the desk and maybe pull your skirt up a bit?' Before I knew it, I found myself starting to do it and then, suddenly, I realised what I was doing and I said, 'No, I am not a glamour puss, I am a union official. If I was a man, would you ask me to sit on the desk and pull my trouser legs up? No.'"

The second thing was that no sooner had Baroness Dean started the job than one of the people who had opposed her started to undermine her by putting all kinds of stories about that were not true: "Stories about my family – saying I did not need the job as I had a private income (not true), saying that I had a beautiful house in an upmarket area – also not true. I realised that I really was in a man's world. But I was determined NOT to become a man."

This was a time when Women's Lib was really taking off and Germaine Greer published *The Female Eunuch*. "All kinds of things were happening but the problem in our industry was that the women who were active (journalists for instance) thought that in order to do a man's job you had to become a surrogate man. I liked to wear nice clothes, nail varnish and lipstick and I did not fulfil their image and so I had a bit of trouble with some of the women as well. Being confronted by that adversity forced me to think about how I was going to do the job."

And then at Christmas a third thing happened. "The newspaper publishers in Manchester had a Christmas party and it was an all-male affair. This was the first time they had a woman officer and I did not get an invitation. So I had to think about what I should do. My deputy had been invited. The party was not in a men's club – it was in a hotel in Manchester so the venue was not a problem. So I decided I had a choice. I could pick up the phone and play hell or I could just go."

So a day or so before the party, Baroness Dean rang the chairman. "I said, 'Looking forward to seeing you at the party tomorrow.' The next day I went and I was scared stiff; I was only young – 34 – and, you know, I had not acquired much confidence even though I had worked with men. This was the next level now. I did not arrive too early; I took a deep breath, walked in the room and focused on the chairman, who was about 6ft 3ins and a true chauvinist. I made a beeline for him. I was very nervous. I walked up to him and said, 'Jack, hello, how are you?' There was absolute silence; he then asked me if I would like a drink, so I said 'Yes'. I realised that I was going to have to go into their world. You cannot expect them to change their world so I had to try to make them feel comfortable with me. Fortunately, the split second of silence was over, everyone carried on and it was fine. At the end I said, 'Well, it didn't fall to pieces did it, Jack?'" (This was Jack Collins, who was managing director of the *Daily Mail* in Manchester in the mid- 1970s.)

So to deal with adversity, Baroness Dean had to take it face on. And she succeeded, but without insulting them. "Looking back," she says, "I did clearly have a strategy. At that time and since then I have met a number of colleagues who are strongly feminist and who are really quite aggressive at times. Back then we had decades of chauvinism, so what do you do? Do you join the club and change it or are you on the outside throwing in bricks? I wanted to join the club and change it. So, if they had a problem with me as a woman who liked being a woman that was their problem – not mine."

In the whole of Baroness Dean's story there are certain key values: "You cannot let go of yourself. I really learnt that in Wapping and also that helped me; the feminists felt they had to go into the pub and drink a pint and go bra-less. Later in my career, the girls I represented in the factories would ask to be able to go home before a meeting to change out of their factory overalls because they had their own pride of appearance too."

So our journey through six key elements in terms of overcoming setbacks is complete. At this stage I would like to thank our contributors for a unique and remarkable set of stories which have so graphically brought this topic to life.

Transformational setbacks are often some of the darker periods in our life. As always in life, there is a balance and synchronicity often provides this. This is the topic of our next chapter.

Synchronicity is sometimes thought of as a new age concept – one that is not real, provable or worthy enough to consider as a 'success attribute'. I have found that if you think in terms of synchronicity allied with alignment, it gives it a direction and purpose. Then the two components have total validity in terms of being part of a DNA of Success.

We have all heard others refer to successful people as 'lucky' or just 'fortunate' to be in the right place at the right time. While that may be true for a very small percentage of successful people, I have found that, while we all need luck, there is often more to it than that. As the famous golfer Gary Player once said, "The harder you try, the luckier you get." I have found that luck can be better represented as the meeting place and outcome of preparation and opportunity. So, within my framework, synchronicity and alignment are the DNA of Success ingredients I see representing this theme.

In this chapter I am going to focus on the stories of our contributors around the emerging theme of synchronicity. We can then look at some research around synchronicity and, coupled with the results of the interviews, we can draw together a nine-point blueprint for this part of the DNA of Success. The chapter is set out in three sections:

- Fascinating stories from seven of our contributors, including Lord MacLaurin's remarkable story of synchronicity at the start of his career with Tesco
- Some research around synchronicity
- A nine-point blueprint to enable synchronicity as a way of leading our lives.

However, as a backdrop to these sections, I have uncovered three guiding principles that are consistent within our contributors' recollections. I believe these will help you as you read through the stories to give a frame of reference:

1. Having a clear end in mind for career and life; a total clarity of purpose. Our contributors all have well-formed views and plans of their life and career goals at a level of detail that makes them real. Early on they had established the start point for their speciality and had a focus and plan.

The magic of synchronicity then seemed to kick in to turn the plans into actual paths and events that formed significant opportunities and life-changing directions in all their lives.

2. Putting ourselves in places and with people who can influence our end in mind. As a memorable line from the movie *Mr Deeds* sums up: "If you want to fly with the eagles, it's no use spending all your time with the turkeys. At least visit the eagle's habitat." A determination to seek out the people and places from which to launch new directions or paths is evident in the lives of our contributors.

3. Synchronicity was a great litmus test of authenticity and of strength of purpose in our contributors. From my interviews it can be seen that if we truly believe in who we are, what we can achieve and how we want to go about this, then synchronicity occurs.

Stories around synchronicity

Every single one of our contributors can relate to this and can trace many occurrences. However, many of them have at least had one major event that was transformational in their careers and lives. This falls into the domain of synchronicity.

Penny Hughes

Penny Hughes definitely recognises the power of synchronicity. She takes up the story that led her to becoming a director for Gap: "When I was at Vodafone I had started to think through my career plan and had set myself a vision of my perfect job." Around this time the Vodafone group was involved in a merger with an American company, AirTouch. It was at this point that Hughes met Don Fisher, the founder of Gap, as Fisher was a non-executive director of AirTouch.

Hughes explains: "From this first chance meeting I was eventually offered the job as an international director of Gap, which was my vision of the perfect job. I can definitely see this as synchronicity and being in the right place at the right time, as I would have had no reason to meet the founder of Gap and there would be no reason for him to come looking for me. It was that being in the right place at the right time that made this happen for me."

Vince Cable

When I spoke to Vince Cable about synchronicity he had an amusing take on this: "For most of my life I seemed to have been in the wrong place! And that is why I only made it into Parliament at the fifth attempt. When I did get in during 1997 at Twickenham, this was about being in the right place at the right time as it was the end of the Tory era. The Liberal Democratic Party had made a national breakthrough under Paddy Ashdown and I was there to take advantage of that."

A second element of synchronicity for Cable came at the end of 2007, when the Northern Rock financial crisis broke during the Liberal Democrats' party conference. Cable explains: "With the focus on the financial crisis and the fact that we were at a major party conference, I became the focus for a number of interviews. My background and acumen in the financial world, and the fact that I had been commenting and warning for years that there was a problem in our financial sector, meant that I now became recognised as someone who had valid comments and experience within the political arena on a subject that was global news. This was September 2007 and following that, when Menzies Campbell stepped down, I became the acting leader."

So it was a combination of the banking crisis and the party leadership that propelled Cable to "celebrity status". He started writing articles for the *Mail on Sunday* and even got to dance with Alesha Dixon on *Strictly Come Dancing*! After that, he had a high profile and started writing his book *The Storm*, about the evolving financial crisis. It became a bestseller and suddenly he was in the national headlines. That was the episode that changed Cable from being a rather obscure MP to having a national presence.

Graham Taylor

Our third contributor to recall synchronicity as a key part of their success is Graham Taylor, who says: "Looking back on my career I can definitely relate to the point when my career changed gear." He had had some success in lower divisions as a young manager and had been offered a job in the top division with a Midlands club, West Bromwich Albion. While deciding whether to take this position, he received a phone call from the chairman of a club in a much lower division, Watford. This chairman turned out to be Sir Elton John.

Taylor explains: "He was so passionate about the ambition and potential for this club that he persuaded me to take over the club. He offered me a five-year contract and I asked him what he would expect during those five years. I expected him to say promotion, maybe one or two divisions. He said 'I would like to get to Europe.' I had two thoughts, the first being 'Are you daft?' and the second, 'What an ambition this man has!'"

Taylor decided to take the job at Watford and this led to eight years of fantastic success. The club moved from the lowest division to top of the top league, at one point eventually finishing second to the team of the decade at the time, Liverpool. Taylor says: "We reached an FA Cup Final and earned a place in the European competition. All this was for less than a million pound net spend, which was remarkably low in terms of spend even in those days. So Elton's dream and ambition became a reality. There would have been no reason for me to have ever embarked on the journey with Watford without the connection to Sir Elton, and it was definitely a life-changing phone call and meeting that eventually led me to becoming the national team manager."

Sir Peter Squire

Sir Peter Squire, who spent his entire career with the Royal Air Force, can also see synchronicity at play within his career, leading him to a life-changing role within the Falklands conflict in the 1980s. Chapter 6 contains an account of his transformational setback when he resigned as squadron leader of the Red Arrows, a world-renowned air display team based in the United Kingdom. On leaving this role, Sir Peter took up the leadership of No.1 Squadron, whose role was with NATO in Europe. This squadron, which had a speciality in air-to-air refuelling, was chosen as the lead force for the Falklands conflict. In Sir Peter's words: "This was a classic case of being in the right place at the right time and, as well as overcoming the disappointment of my Red Arrows experience, being involved in the Falklands conflict definitely accelerated my career and success in the Royal Air Force."

Baroness Dean

Baroness Dean has a remarkable insight into the role that synchronicity played in her success. Her story shows how a national movement and her part in the political and social history of a country propelled her career rapidly forward. She says: "I can definitely relate to synchronicity. For me, the right place and the right time was the mid-1970s. Let me explain that in the early 1970s the public debate about women's rights had really surfaced. Legislation was imminent and a great influence on me, and also a mentor, was Barbara Castle, who was putting political energy into the debate. The women's movement had turned a corner and people's minds were aware of and tuned into women – and women in office and power. So when, having been number two in the union, I put myself forward for the presidency, the timing could not have been better. I am sure I benefited and it helped me win that election and my career really took off. To me, synchronicity is seeing the opportunity and having the courage to take it."

Lord MacLaurin

Lord MacLaurin again has a remarkable story involving synchronicity. In his book *Tiger by the Tail*, which is a fascinating story of his life from Tesco to test cricket, Lord MacLaurin recalls a remarkable time when synchronicity for him actually was the start of his success journey. The story of his first meeting with the founder of Tesco, Jack Cohen, starts in the bar of the Grand Hotel, Eastbourne in the summer of 1959.

"It was one of those places where discretions were as deep as the pile of the carpet, and the Old Malvernian Touring XI were minding their own business over a drink before dinner when this stranger in evening dress drifted up and handed round his card, saying: 'If any of you chaps ever want a job, just give me a call.' The brashness was typical of the man. And for half a century since he had first pushed his barrow out of London's East End, Jack Cohen had been piling it high and selling it cheap and he had become legendary [Jack Cohen was founder and chairman of Tesco]. Not that I was unduly interested in his offer, simply curious as to what made this entrepreneur extraordinaire tick."

On returning home a couple of days later, Lord MacLaurin took up Cohen's offer and gave him a call – to the alarm of his future father-in-law Edgar

Collar, then the deputy chairman of Tesco, who said: "I don't want you to even think about joining the company; I've had so much of the Cohen family, I don't want any of my prospective family coming into the business."

However, Lord MacLaurin continues: "At 23 most of us can be pretty stubborn and I was very determined to see for myself what the 'no-go' of Tesco was really about. I went to meet Jack to satisfy my own curiosity and ended up working for Tesco's and eventually becoming chairman. If I look back on the moment of synchronicity from the bar in Eastbourne, it was as much about knowing that it was the right thing to do to meet Jack Cohen and these paths are put in your life and you need to take them."

Frederick Forsyth

I am going to finish with the story of Frederick Forsyth and how he started on his now globally-acclaimed path as an author, which I believe is one of the most remarkable stories of 'luck' playing a major part in the formation of a career. Forsyth's story starts with a trip to London where he was a provincial newspaper man looking to break into a career in journalism in Fleet Street, then the Mecca of the British Press.

"I had just completed a three-year course created by the National Council for the Training of Journalists and I came to London determined to pursue my career in journalism.

I went up and down Fleet Street and was rebuffed at every lobby I entered. I could not even secure a meeting or interview. So, I decided to take some time out and went to a local pub where I became engaged in a conversation with a gentleman who worked at the Associated Press. We immediately struck up a good rapport as, by chance, he had also worked at the Eastern Daily Press, which was my newspaper in King's Lynn.

He set me up to get my first interview and I met Mr Jarvis, the editor in chief at the Associated Press. Within a few minutes of talking, when he realised I had some language skills, he sent me up a couple of floors to the Reuters office where I met Doon Campbell, who was a legendary editor. He offered me a three-month trial in the office. That was November 1961.

Six month's passed, and in May 1962 the Paris number two developed heart trouble and the decision was taken to fly him home. I replaced him as the junior of the six-man team under the bureau chief. This was the second stroke of luck in six months. I took my two cases and set up in Paris.

This was the Paris of Charles de Gaulle and I attended a number of press conferences as a 'runner' to the writer's bureau chief, Harold King.

Through my time in Paris I got to know Charles de Gaulle's entourage, particularly the French security services. I became very familiar with all the intricacies of the President's life and the threats to it. It became apparent to me that the French rebel forces would not penetrate the security blanket and expertise that the president had surrounding him. All of this fascinated me and led to my thinking and plot for *The Day of the Jackal*."

From provincial newspaper man to meetings in London and Paris, Forsyth's path was certainly paved with chance, luck and synchronicity. Most certainly it was a fascinating journey into his career.

So the stories of seven people certainly support their belief that synchronicity is a criteria for success.

The research and lessons learnt

How can we apply what we have learnt and take it forward from these successes? To answer that question, I wanted to look at the research and then look for commonality and a blueprint that supports our contributors' beliefs around synchronicity. I have found and validated three key reference sources, from completely different disciplines, which give a diverse view of and fascinating insights into synchronicity.

In alignment with Frederick Forsyth and Graham Taylor who have roots emerging from or within journalism, I thought the views of James Redfield, the author of the bestselling novel *The Celestine Prophecy*, would be valid and significant. *The Celestine Prophecy* thrust synchronicity into the public consciousness. As of May 2010, this book had sold over 30 million copies worldwide and had been translated into 34 languages. The book had 165 weeks on the *New York Times* Best Seller list and a film adaptation was released in 2006. Redfield expanded the concept in a series of three sequels, which he completed between 1999 and 2011.

Redfield says that, "All coincidences are significant because they point the way to an unfolding of our personal destiny. By consciously becoming co-creators and choosing what we think, we can have a positive effect on our world. As we focus on our basic life questions, we receive the guidance we need through intuition, dreams, and synchronistic connections that guide us in the direction of our own evolution and transformation."

So, a book that has been acknowledged as a work that elegantly, powerfully and closely aligns fiction with lessons for life seems to support the validity of synchronicity.

For my second reference source, I am working on the principle that research into a topic such as synchronicity should include some link to learned works of psychology. Where better to go than the 'founder' of the term itself, namely Carl Gustav Jung? Jung, a Swiss psychiatrist and an influential thinker, is often considered the first modern psychologist. In fact, his work is behind the most widely used 'personality tool' in use in global business – the Myers Briggs Type Indicator (MBTI) – so his work certainly still has substance, relevance and sustainability in modern business.

Jung defined synchronicity as "the coming together of inner and outer events in a way that cannot be explained by cause and effect and that is meaningful to the observer". Despite spending most of his first seven decades on the planet engaged in deep scientific and analytical work on psychology, Jung became a major source of inspiration in his later life in support of and in rationalising the concept of synchronicity and giving it credibility in the academic world. So I found his acceptance of and work around our DNA attribute of success to be both encouraging and supportive. His quote on this area is, I believe, powerful and insightful.

My third reference source in which I wanted to find quantifiable research is in the work of Charlene Belitz and Meg Lundstrom in their book, *The*

Power of Flow: Practical Ways to Transform Your Life with Meaningful Coincidence. This work contains extensive research and the following extract describes their beliefs and research around synchronicity. Belitz and Lundstrom say: "We experience synchronicity most often when we're open and aware, which in turn is affected by the outer conditions in which we find ourselves and the inner conditions in which we put ourselves. We've concluded that it is possible – through personal choice and action – to enhance flow and accelerate synchronicity."

Their research is among the best I've found in terms of the breadth of people involved from a wide variety of backgrounds and professions. It also turns and focuses the output of the work into everyday language that I feel is understandable, relevant and aligned to my work in this area – and practical in terms of its application to life. So in terms of the research, this is how they describe their approach:

> To understand how synchronicity works, we interviewed 50 people. They ranged in age from 17 to 96 and included lawyers, dancers, secretaries, students, foundation heads, middle managers, therapists, professors, consultants, homemakers, teachers, activists, health professionals, a minister, a rancher and an inventor. We spent absorbing hours with them, delving into why their lives have purpose, inner ease and joyfulness. We asked them about their turning points, their beliefs, their daily practices. We explored why life works so well for them, and what they do day to day to experience flow consciously and consistently.
>
> Valuable information came from two other sources as well. In response to magazine and newspaper articles, hundreds of people from all over the country filled out surveys on their experiences and beliefs. And we organized nine focus groups involving 98 people across the country who hashed through the topics, processes, and techniques we'd learned from the interviews. The surveys and group discussions were transcribed and sorted by subject matter into 241 categories. When printed out – a 12-hour process – the reports filled nearly 1600 pages.

What emerges as the conclusion from this research, and from my interviews, is a set of nine attributes that I believe give us a very powerful framework from which to understand – and just as importantly apply – synchronicity in our lives.

Commitment

If there is only one personal attribute that we need for synchronicity, one that makes everything else possible, it is commitment: commitment to our own growth and expansion, to our family, to our chosen profession, to truth, and to the greatest whole. With commitment, we say 'yes' to life, and we don't just mouth the word. We take a stand for our deepest values, and we do everything it takes to live by them.

Honesty

Honesty, like Janus, the Greek god of hearth and home, has two faces: one that looks outwards and one that faces inwards. Inwardly, as we enter more deeply into flow, we seek integration – the coming together of all of our sometimes-conflicting parts into one powerful whole. This requires a solid commitment to identify and break through layers of misconceptions, self-deceptions, emotional scars, limiting and self-sabotaging beliefs, outdated responses, internal conflicts, buried dreams, hopes and fears – all the accumulated baggage of human existence. We are ruthlessly honest with ourselves, no matter how uncomfortable that may sometimes be. We pursue the truth because we know it will set us free from interference which stops or impairs our ability to be open to the possibilities that exist. We question and probe our own inner world to see what's real, what's true and what's not. The result of this search for the truth is a deep self-understanding and a peace that can come only when we truly know ourselves.

Courage

Courage does not require great feats of daring – it's more about overcoming our fears day in and day out by stepping outside and stretching our personal comfort zone, following our intuition and making ourselves available to the larger plan. It means we overcome our limiting self-beliefs to be open to new information and stretch beyond the way we've always done things in the past. It means we listen within and sometimes turn left when everyone else seems to be going right. It allows us to risk ridicule to create something new, or to risk rejection when we are being true to our sense of what's right.

In my interview with Greg Dyke when we were looking at his values, his quote around courage is aligned perfectly to this point: "Your life is your own. Don't do what others want you to do – do what you want to do. If you get a job and you don't like it, move on. Don't stay; don't sit and moan. You control your own destiny by the courage you display. Do what you believe is right."

Passion
Flow – and through this the possibility of synchronicity – is engendered by passion: passion for life, for knowledge, for a cause, for a relationship, for truth. Passion means caring deeply about something beyond ourselves. It means engaging with it at intense levels. It means letting go of self-protective caution to involve ourselves wholeheartedly with what we love and what we love to do.

Immediacy
Living in flow means living fully in the present. We don't hang out in the past replaying old issues. We don't hang out in the future trying to second-guess how things will turn out. We settle all of our attention on each interaction. We are fully engaged in whatever we are doing, and when time seems rich and full we create a way of being around awareness that allows us to operate from a position of immediacy.

Openness
Being open to a wide range of possibilities makes the power of flow abundant in our daily lives. When we are open, we waste little energy in warding things off; we do not erect walls between ourselves and the outside world. Instead, we embrace whatever develops, for we know that everything we experience has value. Events unfold naturally and effortlessly

because, without preconceptions or judgements, without fear or anger, we are willing to do whatever a situation requires.

Receptivity

Being in flow means that we are receptive to taking our part in the unfolding of events. We listen to our inner voice for messages, we observe all that happens around us – especially synchronicity – and we then move in harmony with the moment. Like a dancer poised in the still moment at the start of a movement, we can go in any direction the music suggests.

Positivity

In positivity, we seek out the value in every situation, at every turn, emphasise it, and work actively with it. That's not to say that we are not aware of or open to the negative potential of a situation; through experience, we've learnt that in the positive side lies the potential for success. We believe everything happens for a reason, and that perfection is found in each moment. As a result, we don't shrink from difficult people or situations or challenges; on the contrary, we move toward them. I sum this up as an unshakeable belief in our ability to succeed – a trait demonstrated reputably by our contributors.

Belief

One thing can switch the experience of flow on and off in an instant: belief and trust in flow itself. This is best summed up in terms of "you will see it when you believe it", rather than the normal version of "I will believe it when I see it", which limits our potential and destroys our opportunity to experience synchronicity.

An insightful quote from the master himself, Albert Einstein, is a good summary to our look at synchronicity as a DNA of Success attribute: "The intellect has little to do on the road to discovery. There comes a leap in consciousness, call it intuition or what you will, the solution comes to you and you don't know how or why."

In conclusion, linking the research and my interviews, I can clearly see a blueprint and a DNA of Success around synchronicity that can be captured and aligned to the nine attributes above. It is a subject that has and will continue to cause heated debate, as people will sit at different points on the continuum on belief around this area. From my interviews, I have found an uncanny consistency and existence of synchronicity 'in play and at work in our lives'. I have captured these in the stories I have uncovered, and I have looked for research to underpin these. It is an area of fascinating possibilities and the ideas in this chapter only serve to open up the subject for you to choose your next steps.

In the final chapter, our contributors reveal which one gift they would pass on from their experience to enable others to achieve success. We then summarise the DNA journey and look at potential next steps for us all.

The aim of this chapter is to summarise, organise and collate the key lessons from the previous chapters into a DNA of Success blueprint. Doing so will not only achieve the primary objective of this book, but it will also provide a practical, applicable and evolutionary set of insights for use as a relevant and personal DNA of Success for all.

To achieve this we will cover three key areas:

- A personal view of and insight on success from each of our contributors in terms of the one gift they would pass on to help others succeed – **the one gift**
- A practical collation of the top three areas of success. This is applied within a DNA of Success intelligence framework. This gives a practical tool for application within the DNA of Success blueprint that can be applied and adopted for our own personal success journey – **the DNA of Success blueprint**
- A summary of and reflections on the emerging themes and output from *The DNA of Success* – **the DNA of Success summary**.

The one gift

The idea behind putting this question to our contributors was to allow them to offer advice around key areas for people to focus on if there was just one area to develop.

Baroness Dean has two: "When I was involved in the Wapping dispute I was often asked what I thought I did right. And I never really came up with the answer myself. However, a great friend of mine, a psychologist, when asked about me, highlighted one of the key gifts for success. 'She listens,' he said." She feels it is an undervalued and neglected skill.

Her second piece of advice is: "Make sure that you know your subject, prepare and read your brief. Too many people believe they can 'surf' through without any depth; you can't. If you skimp in this area you will get found out and it will limit your potential success."

For **Penny Hughes,** it's about sheer hard work: "Work hard, play hard and enjoy what you do. Expect to be tested over a period of time. Look for leadership in your career at every opportunity and don't be afraid to be first at anything."

Inspire people around you but do not try to do their job is **Greg Dyke**'s key message: "You have got to let them get on with it, otherwise the job will drive you mad. Employ good people, keep them enthused, let them get on with it and understand when it does not work. Failure is about 'we' not about 'them'."

He explains: "I think you can take people through grim times but you have to put yourself on the line with them. You have to go and talk to them face to face. We reduced the staff at London Weekend by half, and they still came out liking me because I went to talk to them and I explained why we were doing it. We were generous. If there were particular problems, we would help them. Someone at the London Business School recently said to me, 'I was taught for years that staff don't have to love you, they only have to respect you, but I have changed my mind. Actually they HAVE got to like you. Respect is not enough.'"

Vince Cable believes that "people need to develop a few, but not too many, specialist areas of competence where they become crucially important as they know as much as anyone else. One of the dangers of being in politics is that a lot of people know a little about a lot – that is fine, but there have to be one or two areas where you have such a command that people treat you with respect and come to you for comment or advice. So you have to invest in acquiring real knowledge and expertise in certain areas."

He continues: "I try to be honest – I know that sounds a bit limp, as in politics it is very easy to slip into bad habits, but I do try to be straight with people. A second point is that I do believe in industry and hard work. I have a rather puritanical approach to work. I also believe instinctively in economic fairness. I do not have a particularly ostentatious lifestyle and I think that we would be a better society if we did not have the extremes in luxury and poverty, and if people kept their style of living simpler."

His advice to others regarding success is to be adaptable: "And certainly in a political world it is important to adapt, to be able to listen. I am now in my late sixties but you always have to be prepared to learn and not to rest on your laurels. You have to keep learning constantly."

For **Sir Peter Squire,** it is about helping people to develop the ability to be unwavering and determined to never accept less than the best from themselves or other people they work with. He strongly believes in giving people role models: "My model was a man called John Thomson. I worked directly for Air Chief Marshal Sir John Thomson in three appointments over an eight-year period. He was such an inspiration and mentor and coach to everyone he came in contact with. Good was never enough if you could do better. He had been nominated as the next CAS in 1994, and would almost certainly have gone on to be Chief of the Defence Staff, but, sadly, he died before taking up the CAS appointment."

Graham Taylor values relationships: "You must work at forming and growing relationships. You cannot be successful on your own. You are responsible as a leader for the team success and you must always be accountable. With good relationships you will get great performances from the people whom you lead. Although they are ultimately responsible for their performance, you can motivate them to achieve the best they can. Take care of them and take an interest in the families of the people who work for and with you."

Frederick Forsyth has a very clear view on his gift for success – perseverance: "People rarely succeed at the first time of asking. There are some exceptions and Mark Zuckerberg is obviously an exception to this rule in what he has achieved with Facebook. However, my strong belief is that people who succeed have an innate ability to persevere as a key quality and this includes perseverance through setbacks, perseverance through relationships, and perseverance in looking for the right opportunities in life. Perseverance in my view is a very rare quality, so a focus on this would be my strong advice to anyone looking to increase their chances of success."

So the final words from our contributors focus on, reinforce and validate again several of our key areas of success emerging from the book, that is:

- Perseverance
- Creating winning relationships
- Preparation and the aspiration to be a specialist and to be seen as the best.

The key points from our contributors' summaries can be aligned to three of our chapters and key themes: Perseverance, Creation of Followship (as this needs relationships to work) and Mastery (as this is about specialism and being the best).

We will use these themes as foundation blocks as part of our final blueprint for the DNA of Success.

The DNA of Success blueprint

So far the book has set out seven key areas, with a chapter on each – learning from the best, values and value, creation of followship, mastery, persistence, transformational setbacks, and synchronicity and alignment – and within those, over a hundred topics for success are explored.

In this section, I will be exploring the top three emerging success factors from those seven key areas. I selected these from the summary of our contributors' final input to 'The one gift'. Then, using a success intelligence tool and model, I will apply these to our DNA of Success blueprint and produce a DNA of Success intelligence blueprint.

At the heart of this blueprint is a model based around intelligence. We used the model in Chapter 3 to explore the creation of followship. However, to further expand on this model, its origins and value in terms of a world-class development tool, I would like to give some further background.

As previously mentioned in Chapter 3, I have worked with Mahan Khalsa, the co-founder of the sales performance division within Franklin Covey. Steven Covey, the founder, is a leader and prolific author within the world of personal development. His book, *The 7 Habits of Highly Effective People* is the top-selling business book of all time.

Mahan has a wealth of experience within personal development gained over the last 30 years of working with global clients. Most importantly, he is considered to be a thought leader in terms of the application of knowledge/skills into practical tools that can be used by people to impact on their success. I have developed one of his models and made it relevant, impactful and applicable to our DNA of Success.

In Chapter 3 it was applied in depth to leadership. So, it's clear that it has versatility and adaptability and it gives us a powerful mental model for numerous applications. I have taken this tool and adapted it into a success intelligence model for our summary.

The success intelligence blueprint is built up by looking at three types of intelligence that we all possess. I will summarise the definitions (these are covered in depth in Chapter 3):

- **IQ** – intelligence. This is our intelligence quotient and covers the breadth and depth of our knowledge. It includes our innate, acquired and specialist knowledge learnt and developed throughout our careers and lives.
- **EQ** – emotional intelligence. This is about our relationships and communications which establish connection and meaning with others.
- **PQ** – practical intelligence. This is about how we take our IQ and EQ into life and career situations. It's about how we think and work through life. It covers areas such as clarity of communication, quickness of mind and critical analysis of people and situations. It's about how we get things done.

So, in building our DNA of Success blueprint, my adapted and applied model pulls these three intelligence systems together to produce our success intelligence (quotient) – **SQ**. This gives us the ability to visualise and articulate what we need to develop within each intelligence quotient. (We do this by using the 100+ areas of success defined within this book.) We then know how to develop our success intelligence quotient and therefore develop our blueprint for success. This is represented graphically on the next page as a first-stage, level, and we will now build on this.

DNA Intelligence Model

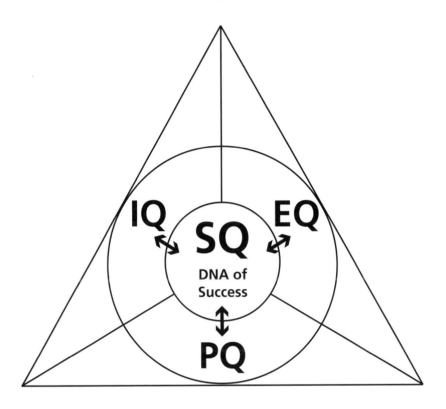

Obviously, choosing just a few factors from over a hundred topic areas, not to mention the multitude of other research and books that cover success, is very challenging. However, as you will see as we build the blueprint, I believe there are a top three if one factor is selected to cover each intelligence 'arm' of the model initially. The contributors also validated these choices in their summaries.

In terms of an **IQ** factor, the one key area emerging is **persistence**. When we covered this in Chapter 5, it showed up constantly and repeatedly as an applied know-how. It also showed itself as a state of mind and a way of being. There is an emergent set of knowledge that can be acquired as a 'how to do' for persistence.

We showed clearly that there were seven key attributes and areas of knowledge in mastering persistence. These can be learnt and then, through our EQ and PQ, applied with both people and situations. Persistence has emerged as a key IQ DNA attribute for success.

One **EQ** success element, the **creation of followship** through leadership covered in Chapter 3, is a recurring mandatory element of success. The chapter covered how our contributors had shown that success is not a singular activity. Their success was and is achieved through and with others. Within the blueprint, EQ could be seen as a fundamental foundation of this creation of followship. A humorous, yet insightful, example of the dancing guy on YouTube was a powerful metaphor for this attribute.

The 20 key areas of EQ emerging both from the work of Goleman, my research and our contributors' insights give this area a practical application and areas of focus for the development of success.

Finally, for a third summary area that focuses on **PQ**, practical intelligence, I have chosen **mastery**, which we covered in Chapter 4. The choice of including this as our practical intelligence element is driven, in my mind, from the viewpoint that the key difference between people who achieve mastery and those who do not is deliberate, repeated practice.

We defined seven component parts and success criteria for mastery, which we then expanded upon. All of these are dependent and interdependent on practical application, practical and repeated practice, and practical goals and feedback. Mastery, we have shown, does not and will not happen without practical focus. PQ is the intelligence quotient that drives this in terms of acquiring success.

Looking now at these three key success factors and linking them to our DNA of Success blueprint, we can represent these within our success intelligence model to give us a practical tool. This enables us to define, apply, master and measure our success journey.

IQ - Persistence
- Definiteness of purpose
- Passion
- Belief
- Definiteness of plans
- Accurate knowledge
- Co-operation

EQ - Creation of Followship
- Self-awareness
- Self-management
- Social awareness
- Emotional skills

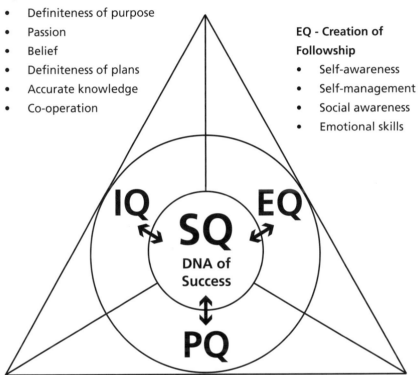

PQ - Mastery
- Deliberate practice
- Defined focus
- Repetition
- Feedback loop
- Engage coach/mentor
- Continuous improvement
- Passion and drive for sustainability

Within the composition of the success blueprint above, I have focused on just three of the emerging major headings. I could have included more. However, its ongoing value as a blueprint is to now move this to a more personal level for ourselves and our own DNA of Success.

You can of course use the model and input from within the 100+ topic areas we have covered in the book. Doing so will allow you to tailor this around your own strengths and areas of development and this will give you your own personal DNA of Success intelligence model. It's about applying all of our 'intelligences' into the success journey. The tools and framework give you a diagnostic and a development path for achievement.

I have found already, having completed the book and in using this model with my clients in a coaching environment, that **it works**. It is practical, versatile and gives outstanding results. Being able to articulate, define and break down success criteria to a detailed level into the three areas of intelligence enables people to work with and towards success. The goal in life is not to be permanently busy, it's to be permanently successful. Using the DNA success model with my clients I have found making that switch to be possible. Success becomes a way of being rather than doing.

I have also tested it with our contributors as a summary of their input and my research and, again, it has been validated. The biggest compliment is that people feel they are able to understand and take definitive action in these areas to drive their personal success. I trust and believe this will be the case as it's applied to your circumstances and when you apply it with others as you focus on your own DNA of Success.

The DNA of Success summary

To conclude the story of *The DNA of Success*, I will go back to what I set out to do and articulated in my introduction.

I was curious and fascinated about what makes people successful and how we could reproduce this success within a DNA that could be understandable, could be articulated and could be applied. The book has produced great stories from great people in an open, honest and sometimes humorous context. Our contributors have given meaningful insights from their successes and from their failures – which is a rare combination. What has clearly emerged from my contributors is that they have integrated success into their lives. However, not at the cost of key relationships, not at the cost of their values and not at the cost of their health or happiness. Their DNA of Success stories have inspired me and allowed me to interpret, research and integrate their successes and failures into my goal of a blueprint to offer my readers. I hope it inspires you and, above all, I trust there is some tangible difference you can take away to help your success.

My objective and drive behind the book was threefold. It was to produce a book that combined an inspirational read with inspirational high-impact, meaningful insights in terms of learning and to produce an inspirational output and blueprint for practical application.

As with every book, the readers will judge whether this has been achieved. I look forward to hearing about your success, your application and your enjoyment of **The DNA of Success**.

References

Chapter 1

Sir Elton John – English singer, composer, pianist. Born 25 March 1947

Charles de Gaulle – French Statesman (22 November 1890–9 November 1970)

Don Keough – Born 1927, retired as president, chief operating officer and a director of the Coca-Cola Company in April 1993

John Smith – British Labour Party politician (13 September 1938–12 May 1994). Leader of the Labour Party, July 1992–May 1994

Sir Basil Embry – Senior Royal Air Force Commander (28 February 1902–7 December 1977). Commander in Chief of Fighter Command, 1949–1953. Author of *Wingless Victory* (Companion Book Club, 1953)

Sir Christopher Gent – Born 10 May 1948, British businessman. Chairman of GlaxoSmithKline plc. He is a non-executive director of Ferrari SpA; a member of KPMG's Chairman Advisory Group; a Senior Adviser at Bain & Co; and a member of the Advisory Board of Reform. Former Chief Executive Officer of Vodafone Group plc and Mannesmann AG, and Director of Network Services at International Computers Limited (ICL)

Dame Anita Roddick – British businesswoman, founder of the Body Shop. The Body Shop has over 1980 stores, more than 77 million customers and operates in 50 markets and 25 languages

Sir John Edward Cohen – British businessman (6 October 1898–24 March 1979). Born Jacob Edward Kohen and commonly known as Jack Cohen. He founded the Tesco supermarket chain

Derek Williams – former Managing Director of Coca-Cola Schweppes

Joe Sheridan – Past Secretary of the Manchester Branch of SOGAT

George Booth – Brenda Dean's mentor and teacher in Salford

Zig Ziglar – Born 6 November 1926, American author, salesman and motivational speaker

Rupert Murdoch – Born 11 March 1931, Australian-American media mogul, Chairman and CEO of News Corporation

Richard Branson – Born 18 July 1950, British Baron, founder and owner of the Virgin Group. Author of *Business Stripped Bare: Adventures of a Global Entrepreneur* (Virgin Books, 2008)

Chapter 2

Robert Maxwell – Czechoslovakian-born British media proprietor and former Member of Parliament (10 June 1923–5 November 1991)

Ralph Waldo Emerson – American lecturer, essayist and poet (1803–1882)

Oscar Wilde – Irish writer and poet (16 October 1854–30 November 1900)

War Graves Commission – Established by Royal Charter in 1917. Non-profit making organisation founded by Sir Fabian Ware

Imperial War Museum – partially government-funded museum covering conflicts from First World War to today

Dell Computer Corporation – is an American multinational information technology corporation based in Round Rock, Texas, that develops, sells and supports computers and related products and services. Bearing the name of its founder, Michael Dell, the company is one of the largest technological corporations in the world

Vodafone – Vodafone Group plc is a global telecommunications company headquartered in London and Newbury. It is the world's largest mobile telecommunications company measured by revenues and the world's second-largest measured by subscribers (behind China Mobile), with around 341 million subscribers as of November 2010. It operates networks and has partner networks in over 70 countries. It owns 45% of Verizon Wireless, the largest mobile telecommunications company in the USA. The name Vodafone reflects the provision of voice and data services over mobile phones. Its primary listing is on the London Stock Exchange and it is a constituent of the FTSE100 index. It had a market capitalisation of approximately £93 billion, making it the fourth-largest company on the London Stock Exchange

BP – BP is one of the world's leading international oil and gas companies, providing its customers with fuel for transportation, energy for heat and light, retail services and petrochemicals products. As at December 2010, sales were at $297 billion and BP employed just short of 80,000 people and were active in 29 countries

Skype – is a software application that allows users to make voice and video calls over the Internet. Calls to other users within the Skype service are free, while calls to both traditional landline telephones and mobile phones can be made for a fee using a debit-based user account system. Skype has also become popular for its additional features, which include instant messaging, file transfer and video conferencing. Skype had 663 million registered users as of 2010. The network is operated by Skype Limited, which has its headquarters in Luxembourg

BBC – The British Broadcasting Corporation (BBC) is a British public service broadcaster, headquartered at Broadcasting House in the City of Westminster, London. It is the largest broadcaster in the world, with 23,000 staff. Its main responsibility is to provide public service broadcasting in the United Kingdom, Channel Islands and Isle of Man. The BBC is an autonomous public service broadcaster operates under a Royal Charter and a Licence and Agreement from the Home Secretary. Within the UK, its work is funded principally by an annual television licence fee, which is charged to all households, companies and organisations using any type of equipment to record and/or receive live television broadcasts; the level of the fee is set annually by the British government and agreed by Parliament

Bill Clinton – Born 14 August 1946, American politician, former 42nd President of the United States of America

Chapter 3

Daniel Goleman – Born 7 March 1946, author, psychologist and science journalist. Author of *Emotional Intelligence* (Bloomsbury, 1995)

YouTube – Sasquatch Music Festival 2009

Robert Holden, PhD – Director of 'The Happiness Project' and 'Success Intelligence'

Oprah Winfrey – Host of *Good Morning America*, plus two BBC television documentaries

Napoleon Hill – American author (26 October 1883–8 November 1970). Wrote *Think and Grow Rich* (Ralston Society, 1937)

Jack Welch – Born 19 November 1935, American chemical engineer, businessman and author. Former Chairman and CEO of General Electric. Author of *Jack: Straight from the Gut* (Business Plus, 2001)

Harry S Truman – 33rd President of the United States of America (8 May 1884–26 December 1972)

Dr Norman Vincent Peale – Minister and author (31 May 1898–24 December 1993). Wrote *The Power of Positive Thinking* (Ballentine Books, 1996)

Chapter 4

Sir Victor Blank – Born 1942, prominent British businessman. Co-author of *Weinberg & Blank on Take-overs and Mergers*

Peter Thomson – Strategist. Producer of audio publication, *The Achiever's Edge*

Chapter 5

Andrew Carnegie – Scottish-American industrialist, businessman, entrepreneur and philanthropist (25 November 1835–11 August 1919)

Jamie Smart – British Neuro-Linguistic Programming trainer. Managing Director of Salad – an NLP training company

Leonard Orr – Born circa 1938, American best known for developing Rebirthing-Breathwork

Robert Anton Wilson – American author (18 January 1932–11 January 2007). Wrote *Prometheus Rising* (New Falcon Publications, 1988)

Henry Ford – American Industrialist, founder of Ford Motor Company (30 July 1863–7 April 1947)

Chapter 6

Nelson Mandela – Born 18 July 1918, former President of South Africa. Anti-apartheid activist

Alastair Campbell – Born 25 May 1957, British journalist, broadcaster, political aide and author

The Hutton Report – 2003 Judicial Inquiry chaired by Lord Hutton – appointed by Labour government to investigate circumstances surrounding death of David Kelly

David Kelly – British scientist and expert on biological warfare (14 May 1944–17 July 2003). Formerly a United Nations weapons inspector in Iraq

Red Arrows – Royal Air Force Aerobatic Team based at RAF Scampton, soon to be moved to RAF Waddington. Formed in late 1964

The Nigerian Biafran War – Political conflict as result of economic, ethnic, cultural and religious tensions among various peoples of Nigeria (6 July 1967–15 January 1970)

British High Commissioner in Lagos – Senior British diplomat based in Lagos

Thomas Edison – American inventor, scientist and businessman (11 February 1847–18 October 1931). Best known for developing the phonograph, the motion picture camera and the electric light bulb

Joe Sheriden – British union leader

Germaine Greer – Born 29 January 1939, Australian writer, academic, journalist and scholar. Widely regarded as one of the most significant feminist voices of the late 20th century

Jack Collins – Managing Director of the *Daily Mail* in Manchester in the mid-1970s

Chapter 7

Don Fisher – American businessman who founded The Gap clothing stores (3 September 1928–27 September 2009).

Northern Rock plc – British bank best known for becoming the first bank in 150 years to suffer a bank run after having had to approach the Bank of England for a loan facility.

Sir Menzies Campbell MP – Born 22 May 1941, British politician and advocate, and a retired sprinter. Former Leader of the Liberal Democrats

West Bromwich Albion – English Premier League Association Football Club, formed in 1878

NATO – North Atlantic Treaty Organization – an intergovernmental military alliance based on the North Atlantic Treaty, which was signed on 4 April 1949

Edgar Collar – former Deputy Chairman of Tesco

James Redfield – Born 19 March 1950, American author, lecturer, screenwriter and film producer. Noted for his novel *The Celestine Prophecy* (Warner Books, 1997)

Gustav Jung – Swiss psychiatrist, an influential thinker and founder of Analytical Psychology (26 July 1875–6 June 1961)

Charlene Belitz and Meg Lundstrom – authors of *The Power of Flow: Practical Ways to Transform Your Life with Meaningful Coincidence* (Crown Publications, 1999, first edition)

Janus – The Greek God of Hearth

Albert Einstein – German-born theoretical physicist who developed the theory of general relativity (14 March 1879–18 April 1955)

I recommend the following list of books for further inspiration on success; these are referenced in this book:

Belitz, C. and Lundstrom, M. *The Power of Flow: Practical Ways to Transform Your Life with Meaningful Coincidence*. London: Harmony Books, 2007

Cable, V. *The Storm*. London: Atlantic Books, 2009

Collins, J. *Good to Great*. London: Random House Business Books, 2001

Colvin, G. *Talent is Overrated*. London: Penguin Group, 2008

Covey, S. *The 7 Habits of Highly Effective People*. New York: Simon and Schuster, 1989

Goleman, D. *Emotional Intelligence*. New York: Bantam, 1995

Hill, N. *Think and Grow Rich*. London: Ballantine Books, 1996

Holden, R. *Success Intelligence*. London: Hay House Publishers, 2008

Jung, C. *Synchronicity*. Princeton, NJ: Princeton University Press, 1969

MacLaurin, Lord, I. *Tiger by the Tail*. Basingstoke: Macmillan, 1999

Other recommended reading that hasn't been specifically mentioned:

Borg, J. *Persuasion: The Art of Influencing People*. Englewood Cliffs, NJ: Prentice Hall, 2010

Cialdini, Dr. R. *Influence: Science and Practice*. Cambridge: Pearson, 2009

Collins, J. *How the Mighty Fall*. London: Random House Business Books, 2010

Dean, Baroness B. *Hot Mettle: Sogat, Murdoch and Me*. London: Politico's Publishing Ltd, 2007

Dyke, G. *Inside Story*. London: Harper Perennial, 2010

Fine, A. *You Already Know How To Be Great*. New York: Portfolio Penguin, 2010

Holden, R. *Happiness Now*. London: Hay House, 1997

Hooper, A. and Potter, J. *Intelligent Leadership*. London: Random House, 2000

O'Neil, J.P. *The Paradox of Success*. New York: Tarcher, 1994

Parker, C. *The Thinkers 50*. London: Business Press, 2006

Renshaw, B. *Successful but Something Missing*. London: Rider, 2000

Roddick, A. *Business as Unusual*. London: Thorsons, 2000

Semler, R. *The Seven-day Weekend*. North Idaho, ID: Century, 2003

Williams, N. *Unconditional Success*. New York: Bantam, 2002